ARSENAL

FC

Trivia

A Selection of Incredible Trivia Tests and Interesting Information for Serious Gunners Fans!

CONTENT

PART 1

ARSENAL FC - THE LEGACY

CHAPTER 1

A Brief History of Arsenal FC

From Dial Square to Global Giant: A Deep Dive into Arsenal FC's History

Arsenal Football Club, a name synonymous with English football, is more than just a team; it's an institution woven into the fabric of London and a global phenomenon. This essay will embark on a detailed journey through the club's rich history, exploring the pivotal moments, influential figures, and enduring legacy that have shaped Arsenal into the giant it is today.

Humble Beginnings: The Dial Square Era (1886-1893)

The story begins in the smoky, industrial landscape of late 19th century Woolwich, Southeast London. Within the walls of the Royal Arsenal armaments factory, a group of workers, led by the ambitious Scotsman David Danskin, sought a recreational outlet amidst the grime and toil. In October 1886, they gathered at the Royal Oak pub, pooling their meager resources to purchase a football and establish Dial Square, named after a workshop within the factory. This act of camaraderie and shared passion marked the genesis of Arsenal Football Club.

Dial Square played its first match on 11th December 1886 against Eastern Wanderers, a game that ended in a 6-0 victory. This early success fueled the team's ambition, and soon, the name was changed to Royal Arsenal, reflecting a growing sense of identity and pride. Playing on a makeshift pitch within the factory grounds, the team competed in various local leagues and cup competitions, gradually gaining recognition for its attacking flair and competitive spirit.

A pivotal moment arrived in 1891 when Royal Arsenal won the Kent Senior Cup and the London Charity Cup, demonstrating its growing prowess. This success, coupled with the increasing professionalism creeping into the game, prompted the club to take a bold step. In 1893, Royal Arsenal became Woolwich Arsenal and transitioned to a professional entity, a decision that would have far-reaching consequences for the club's future.

The Move North and Rise to Prominence (1893-1925):

Woolwich Arsenal's entry into the Football League Second Division in 1893 marked a significant milestone. However, the club's geographical isolation in Southeast London proved to be a hindrance. Despite on-field progress, attracting larger crowds and generating sufficient revenue proved challenging. Recognizing this, ambitious businessman and chairman Henry Norris orchestrated a daring move in 1913, relocating the club to Highbury, North London.

This strategic decision proved to be a masterstroke. Highbury, with its readily accessible location and burgeoning football fanbase, provided fertile ground for Arsenal to flourish. The move also coincided with the club dropping "Woolwich" from its name, becoming simply "Arsenal," signifying a new era and a broader appeal. While relegation to the Second Division followed in 1913, it proved to be a temporary setback. Arsenal returned to the First Division in 1919, and the foundations for future success were firmly laid.

The Chapman Revolution: A Blueprint for Modern Football (1925-1934):

The appointment of Herbert Chapman as manager in 1925 ushered in a golden era for Arsenal. Chapman, a visionary tactician and astute administrator, revolutionized the club both on and off the pitch. He introduced the groundbreaking "WM" formation, a tactical system that provided defensive solidity while unleashing attacking flair, and implemented modern training methods, emphasizing fitness, discipline, and scientific approaches.

Chapman's impact was immediate and profound. In 1930, Arsenal won its first major trophy, the FA Cup, defeating Huddersfield Town 2-0 in the final. This triumph was followed by the club's first league title in 1931, achieved with a record-breaking 127 goals scored. Chapman continued to build a dominant team, securing another league title in 1933 and further refining his tactical innovations.

Chapman's influence extended beyond trophies. He rebranded the club, modernized the Highbury stadium with the iconic East Stand and introduced floodlights, and even lobbied for the renaming of the local Underground station from "Gillespie Road" to "Arsenal." Tragically, Chapman died suddenly in 1934, but his legacy as one of the game's most influential figures remains firmly entrenched in Arsenal's DNA.

Maintaining the Momentum: Post-Chapman and Mid-Century Success (1934-1966):

Following Chapman's untimely death, his assistants Joe Shaw and George Allison maintained the winning momentum. Arsenal secured back-to-back league titles in 1934 and 1935, and another in 1938, cementing their status as the dominant force in English football. The outbreak of World War II brought football to a halt, but Arsenal emerged from the conflict with renewed determination.

The post-war era saw continued success, with league titles in 1948 and 1953, and an FA Cup triumph in 1950. However, the following decades proved to be a period of relative inconsistency. Despite boasting talented players like Danny Clapton and Joe Baker, and enjoying occasional cup success, such as the Inter-Cities Fairs Cup in 1970, a sustained period of dominance proved elusive.

The Wenger Revolution: A New Era of Dominance (1996-2018):

The arrival of Arsène Wenger in 1996 marked a watershed moment in Arsenal's history. The Frenchman, relatively unknown at the time, brought with him a revolutionary approach to the game, emphasizing attacking football, meticulous preparation, and the development of young talent. Wenger's impact was transformative, ushering in an era of unprecedented success and establishing Arsenal as a global force.

Wenger inherited a talented squad and immediately set about implementing his philosophy. He revolutionized training methods, introduced new dietary and fitness regimes, and placed a strong emphasis on scouting and youth development. The results were spectacular. In 1998, Arsenal won the Premier League and FA Cup double, a feat repeated in 2002.

The pinnacle of Wenger's reign came in the 2003-04 season, when Arsenal achieved the unthinkable, going an entire league season unbeaten. This remarkable achievement, dubbed "The Invincibles," cemented Wenger's status as a managerial great and etched the names of players like Thierry Henry, Patrick Vieira, Dennis Bergkamp, and Robert Pires into Arsenal folklore.

Wenger's reign also saw Arsenal dominate the FA Cup, winning the trophy a record seven times, including a memorable victory over

Chelsea in the 2017 final. Furthermore, he guided the club to its first-ever Champions League final in 2006, narrowly losing to Barcelona in a dramatic encounter.

Beyond trophies, Wenger's legacy lies in his commitment to attractive, attacking football and his influence on the development of the modern game. He transformed Arsenal into a global brand, oversaw the move from Highbury to the Emirates Stadium, and left an indelible mark on the club's culture and identity.

The Modern Era: Navigating New Challenges (2018-Present):

Following Wenger's departure in 2018, Arsenal has entered a new chapter in its history. While the club has faced challenges in replicating the consistent success of the Wenger era, there have been signs of progress. Under current manager Mikel Arteta, a former Arsenal captain under Wenger, the team has shown promise, winning the FA Cup in 2020 and demonstrating a renewed commitment to attacking football.

The current era is one of transition and rebuilding. Arsenal is striving to compete at the highest level while maintaining its core values and traditions. The club's history, with its tales of triumph, innovation, and unwavering community spirit, provides a guiding light as it navigates the challenges of the modern game.

Arsenal's journey from a humble workers' team to a global giant is a testament to the enduring power of community, ambition, and innovation. The club's history is etched in the hearts of millions, and its future is filled with promise. As Arsenal continues to evolve and adapt, one thing remains certain: the spirit of Dial Square will forever burn brightly within the soul of this iconic club.

Notebook Prompt: Use this space to jot down any new facts about football you learned from this section or ideas to share with other fans. You can also jot down any questions you have about these rules or how they apply in different game situations.

CHAPTER 2

Arsenal's Global Fanbase

Arsenal FC: A Global Tapestry of Gooners - A Deeper Dive

Arsenal Football Club's impact extends far beyond the confines of North London, weaving a vibrant tapestry of support that spans continents and cultures. This article delves deeper into the fascinating world of Arsenal's global fanbase, exploring its origins, its diverse manifestations, and the club's multifaceted efforts to connect with its international supporters.

Tracing the Roots of Global Support:

While Arsenal's global fanbase has exploded in recent decades, the seeds of its international appeal were sown much earlier. The club's historical commitment to attacking, aesthetically pleasing football, often referred to as "the Arsenal way," has resonated with fans across the globe who appreciate the artistry and beauty of the game.

Furthermore, Arsenal's success in the 1930s under Herbert Chapman, and its subsequent periods of dominance, helped establish the club as a force to be reckoned with on the international stage. The emergence of iconic players like Dennis Bergkamp, Thierry Henry, and Patrick Vieira in the late 1990s and early 2000s further cemented

Arsenal's global appeal, attracting a new generation of fans who admired the club's style of play and its commitment to developing world-class talent.

A Global Mosaic of Supporters' Clubs:

Arsenal's global fanbase is brought to life through a vast network of official supporters' clubs, each with its own unique character and story. These clubs serve as local hubs for Gooners, providing a sense of community and belonging for fans far from North London.

- **In Africa:** The Arsenal Nigeria Supporters' Club, one of the largest and most active in the world, boasts thousands of members who gather in vibrant viewing centers across the country to cheer on their beloved team. Similarly, the Arsenal Kenya Supporters' Club organizes regular meet-ups, social events, and charity initiatives, fostering a strong sense of community among Kenyan Gooners.

- **In Asia:** The Arsenal Singapore Supporters' Club, with its dedicated committee and active membership, provides a platform for Singaporean fans to connect, organize match viewings, and participate in social events. The Arsenal Vietnam Supporters' Club, known for its passionate displays of support, has gained recognition for its creative chants and tifos, showcasing the vibrant fan culture in Vietnam.

- **In North America:** The Arsenal America supporters' club, with branches in numerous cities across the United States and Canada, provides a welcoming space for North American Gooners to connect and share their passion for the club. From organized watch parties to participation in local soccer leagues, these clubs foster a strong sense of community and camaraderie.

- **In Europe:** Beyond the UK, Arsenal boasts a strong following across Europe. The Arsenal Norway Supporters' Club, for example, organizes trips to London for matches, fostering a direct connection with the club and its home ground.

These are just a few examples of the hundreds of Arsenal supporters' clubs that exist worldwide. Each club contributes to the global mosaic of Gooners, adding its unique flavor and passion to the worldwide community.

Bringing the Arsenal Experience to the World: A History of International Tours:

Arsenal has a long and storied history of embarking on international pre-season tours, bringing the team closer to its global fanbase and expanding its reach into new markets. These tours not only generate significant revenue but also play a crucial role in building relationships with fans and sponsors in key international markets.

- **Asian Adventures:** Arsenal has toured extensively in Asia, recognizing the immense popularity of the club in the region. The 2017 pre-season tour saw the team play in front of packed stadiums in Sydney, Shanghai, and Beijing, demonstrating the fervent support for the club in these cities. In 2013, the club visited Indonesia, Vietnam, and Japan, engaging with local fans and participating in community events.

- **African Outreach:** Arsenal has also made significant efforts to connect with its African fanbase. In 2013, the team visited Nigeria, playing a friendly match against the Nigerian national team in Abuja. This visit generated immense excitement and further solidified the club's strong following in the country.

- **American Expansion:** Arsenal has regularly toured the United States, recognizing the growing popularity of soccer in the country. The club has participated in the International Champions Cup, a pre-season tournament featuring top European teams, playing matches in cities like Los Angeles, New York, and Washington D.C.

These international tours provide a unique opportunity for fans around the world to witness their heroes in action and experience the excitement of Arsenal firsthand. They also allow the club to engage with local communities, participate in cultural exchanges, and further strengthen its global brand.

Global Partnerships: Beyond the Pitch:

Arsenal's global partnerships extend beyond commercial sponsorships, encompassing initiatives that promote social change and raise awareness of important issues.

- **Visit Rwanda:** The partnership with Visit Rwanda, launched in 2018, is a prime example of Arsenal's commitment to using its global platform for positive social impact. This collaboration aims to promote Rwanda as a tourist destination and highlight the country's remarkable progress and development. The "Visit Rwanda" logo features prominently on Arsenal's shirt sleeves, providing global visibility for the country and generating significant interest in its tourism sector.

- **Save the Children:** Arsenal has a long-standing partnership with Save the Children, a global charity dedicated to improving the lives of children around the world. The club has supported various Save the Children initiatives, including fundraising campaigns and awareness-raising events, leveraging its global reach to make a positive impact on children's lives.

These partnerships demonstrate Arsenal's commitment to using its global platform for good, extending its influence beyond the football pitch and contributing to positive social change.

Connecting with International Fans: A Multi-Faceted Approach:

Arsenal employs a multi-faceted approach to connect with its international fanbase, utilizing digital platforms, fan initiatives, and localized content to engage with supporters around the world.

- **Digital Engagement:** The club's official website and social media platforms provide a constant stream of content tailored to different regions and languages. Arsenal's dedicated Chinese social media accounts, for example, offer exclusive content for the vast Chinese fanbase, while the Arsenal USA website caters specifically to the American audience.
- **Fan Initiatives:** The "Arsenal Gap Year" program offers young fans the opportunity to spend a year working at the club, gaining valuable experience and immersing themselves in the Arsenal culture. The club also runs coaching clinics and soccer schools in various countries, providing young players with the opportunity to learn from experienced coaches and develop their skills.
- **Localized Content:** Arsenal produces localized content for specific regions, including dedicated websites, social media

accounts, and fan magazines. This ensures that fans around the world have access to relevant and engaging content in their preferred language.

These efforts demonstrate Arsenal's commitment to connecting with its diverse fanbase and providing a personalized experience for supporters around the world.

The Impact of a Global Community:

The global reach of Arsenal's fanbase has a profound impact on the club, both on and off the pitch. The passionate support from international fans creates a vibrant atmosphere at matches, both at the Emirates Stadium and during away games. This global support also translates into significant revenue for the club through merchandise sales, sponsorship deals, and broadcasting rights.

Furthermore, Arsenal's global fanbase plays a crucial role in promoting the club's values and contributing to its social impact. Supporters' clubs around the world engage in charitable activities, raising funds for local causes and supporting community initiatives. The club's global partnerships, such as the Visit Rwanda collaboration, also contribute to positive social change and raise awareness of important issues.

Conclusion:

Arsenal Football Club's global fanbase is a testament to the unifying power of sport. From London to Lagos, Tokyo to Toronto, the Gooners form a passionate and dedicated community that transcends geographical boundaries. The club's efforts to connect with its international supporters, through tours, partnerships, and digital engagement, have created a truly global family. As Arsenal continues to evolve and compete on the world stage, its global fanbase will undoubtedly play a crucial role in its future success, both on and off the pitch. The tapestry of Gooners, woven from diverse cultures and united by a shared passion, is a testament to the enduring legacy of this iconic club.

Notebook Prompt: Use this space to jot down any new facts about football you learned from this section or ideas to share with other fans. You can also jot down any questions you have about these rules or how they apply in different game situations.

....

....

....

....

....

....

....

....

....

....

....

....

....

CHAPTER 3

Arsenal's Identity and Culture

More Than a Club: A Deep Dive into Arsenal's Identity and Culture

Arsenal Football Club is more than just a team that graces the pitch; it is an institution woven into the fabric of North London and a global phenomenon that resonates with millions worldwide. This chapter embarks on a comprehensive exploration of Arsenal's identity and culture, delving into the historical nuances, iconic symbols, and unwavering values that have shaped the club's unique character and enduring legacy.

The Fabric of Tradition: Symbols and Rituals

Arsenal's identity is intricately linked to a rich tapestry of traditions and symbols, passed down through generations of supporters, creating a powerful sense of belonging and shared identity that transcends geographical boundaries.

- **The Red and White:** A Tale of Two Cities: The club's iconic red and white kit is instantly recognizable across the globe, a visual embodiment of Arsenal's history and values. The story behind the colours is a fascinating tale that links Arsenal to another historic club, Nottingham Forest. In 1886, Dial Square, the nascent Arsenal, lacked a proper kit. Fred

Beardsley and Morris Bates, two founding members who had previously played for Nottingham Forest, wrote to their former club seeking assistance. Forest responded generously, donating a set of their red shirts. This act of camaraderie marked the beginning of Arsenal's association with the colour red. The white sleeves were added later, possibly inspired by the white shirts worn by local team, Woolwich Albion. This combination of red and white has become synonymous with Arsenal, representing its heritage, passion, and unwavering spirit.

- **Victoria Concordia Crescit:** Unity in the Pursuit of Victory: The club's Latin motto, "Victory Through Harmony," encapsulates Arsenal's philosophy of teamwork, unity, and the collective pursuit of success. These words, emblazoned on the club crest, serve as a constant reminder of the values that underpin Arsenal's identity. The motto emphasizes the importance of collaboration, mutual respect, and the belief that success is achieved through the harmonious efforts of the entire team, both on and off the pitch.

- **Iconic Chants:** The Soundtrack of Arsenal: The Emirates Stadium comes alive with the passionate chants of Arsenal supporters, creating an electrifying atmosphere that is unique to the club. These chants, passed down through generations, are more than just songs; they are expressions of loyalty, pride, and unwavering support, forming an integral part of the Arsenal matchday experience.

    - **"One-Nil to the Arsenal":** This classic chant, often accompanied by a rhythmic clapping, is a declaration of confidence and a celebration of Arsenal's attacking prowess.
    - **"We've got Özil":** This chant, dedicated to the

German playmaker Mesut Özil, highlights the fans' appreciation for individual brilliance and their ability to recognize and celebrate exceptional talent.
    - **"She Wore a Yellow Ribbon":** This traditional song, adapted by Arsenal fans, is a testament to the club's enduring connection with its supporters and the sense of community that binds them together.
    - **"Boring, Boring Arsenal":** Originally chanted ironically by opposition fans during George Graham's defensively solid era, this chant has been reclaimed by Arsenal supporters, often used humorously to celebrate a hard-fought victory or a moment of defensive resilience.
- **The Clock End: The Heartbeat of Highbury:** Though the physical Clock End no longer exists at the Emirates Stadium, its spirit lives on in the hearts of Arsenal fans. This iconic stand at Highbury, known for its passionate and vocal supporters, represented the soul of the club, a symbol of unwavering loyalty and unwavering support. The Clock End was where the most dedicated Gooners congregated, creating an atmosphere of fervent support that often spurred the team on to victory. Even today, the term "Clock End faithful" evokes a sense of nostalgia and admiration for the unwavering dedication of Arsenal's most passionate supporters.

Highbury and the Emirates: Homes of Arsenal

The physical spaces where Arsenal has played its home matches have become integral to the club's identity, each stadium holding a unique place in the hearts of supporters and representing different eras in the club's history.

- **Highbury:** The Home of Football: For over 93 years,

Highbury was more than just a stadium; it was a cathedral of football, a place where legends were made and memories were etched into the hearts of generations of fans. The iconic marble halls, the Art Deco East Stand, and the intimate atmosphere created a unique sense of belonging and tradition.

- **The Marble Halls:** These grand entrance halls, with their elegant marble staircase and ornate decorations, exuded a sense of history and grandeur, welcoming players and fans alike into a special place.
- **The East Stand:** This iconic stand, with its distinctive Art Deco design, was a symbol of Highbury's elegance and architectural significance. It housed the Directors' Box and provided a privileged view of the action for the club's most esteemed guests.
- **The North Bank:** This towering stand, known for its steep incline and passionate supporters, created an intimidating atmosphere for visiting teams. The North Bank was a cauldron of noise and energy, a testament to the unwavering support of Arsenal's faithful.

Highbury was not just a ground; it was a home, a symbol of Arsenal's history and heritage, a place where generations of Gooners shared their passion for the club.

- **Emirates Stadium:** A Modern Marvel: The move to the Emirates Stadium in 2006 marked a new era for Arsenal. This state-of-the-art stadium, with its increased capacity and modern facilities, provided a platform for the club to grow and compete at the highest level.

    - **Increased Capacity:** The Emirates Stadium boasts a capacity of over 60,000, significantly larger than Highbury, allowing more fans to experience the thrill of watching Arsenal live.

- **Modern Facilities:** The stadium features state-of-the-art facilities, including comfortable seating, spacious concourses, and a wide range of food and beverage options, enhancing the matchday experience for supporters.
- **The "Arsenalisation" Process:** The club has made significant efforts to infuse the Emirates Stadium with the spirit and traditions of Highbury. Statues of club legends, murals depicting iconic moments, and the preservation of historical artifacts help create a sense of continuity and connection with the club's past.

While the transition from Highbury was emotional for many fans, the Emirates has become a symbol of Arsenal's ambition and its commitment to progress, providing a modern home for the club and its ever-growing global fanbase.

Innovation: A Legacy of Pushing Boundaries

Throughout its history, Arsenal has been at the forefront of innovation, both on and off the pitch. The club has consistently embraced new ideas and technologies, pushing the boundaries of the game and setting new standards for others to follow.

- **The Chapman Revolution:** A Pioneer of Modern Football: Herbert Chapman, Arsenal's legendary manager in the 1920s and 30s, was a true visionary who revolutionized the game with his innovative tactics and modern approach to management.

    - **The "WM" Formation:** Chapman's introduction of the "WM" formation was a tactical masterstroke. This system, with its emphasis on defensive solidity and attacking fluidity, dominated English football for decades and laid the foundation for modern tactical approaches.

- **Modern Training Methods:** Chapman was a pioneer in implementing modern training methods, emphasizing fitness, discipline, and scientific approaches. He introduced new training drills, dietary regimes, and even physiotherapy techniques, transforming the way players prepared for matches.
- **Stadium Innovations:** Chapman also oversaw significant improvements to Highbury stadium, including the construction of the iconic East Stand and the introduction of floodlights, enhancing the matchday experience for fans and demonstrating the club's commitment to progress.

- **Wenger's Influence:** A New Era of Innovation: Arsène Wenger, Arsenal's longest-serving manager, brought a new wave of innovation to the club, further solidifying its reputation as a forward-thinking institution.

  - **Scientific Approach:** Wenger revolutionized training methods, introducing new dietary and fitness regimes, and placing a strong emphasis on sports science and data analysis. He transformed the way players trained and prepared for matches, contributing to the development of the modern game.
  - **Youth Development:** Wenger placed a strong emphasis on scouting and youth development, establishing Arsenal's academy as one of the best in the world. He nurtured young talents like Cesc Fàbregas, Robin van Persie, and Jack Wilshere, shaping them into world-class players.
  - **Attacking Philosophy:** Wenger's commitment to attacking, aesthetically pleasing football further solidified Arsenal's reputation as a forward-thinking

club. His teams played with flair and creativity, captivating fans around the world and influencing a generation of coaches and players.

- **Technological Advancements:** Embracing the Digital Age: Arsenal has embraced technology to gain a competitive edge, utilizing data analysis and scouting tools to enhance its performance on the pitch.
    - **Performance Analysis:** The club's Performance Analysis department utilizes advanced analytics and data visualization tools to analyze player performance, identify tactical trends, and scout potential signings. This data-driven approach helps the club make informed decisions and stay ahead of the curve.
    - **StatDNA:** Arsenal acquired StatDNA, a data analysis company, in 2012, further enhancing its analytical capabilities. This technology allows the club to analyze vast amounts of data, identify patterns, and make informed decisions regarding player recruitment and tactical approaches.
    - **Scouting Network:** Arsenal has a global scouting network that utilizes technology to identify and assess potential signings. Scouting software and video analysis tools allow the club to efficiently evaluate players from around the world, ensuring that it can compete for the best talent.

The Arsenal Foundation: Community Engagement and Social Impact

Arsenal's identity extends beyond the football pitch, encompassing a strong commitment to community engagement and social impact. The Arsenal Foundation, the club's charitable arm, plays a vital role in supporting local communities and making a positive difference in the lives of young people.

- **Local Initiatives:** Making a Difference in North London: The Arsenal Foundation runs a variety of programs in North London, focusing on education, social inclusion, and youth development.

    - **The "Arsenal Hub":** This community hub provides a safe and supportive environment for young people, offering educational workshops, sports activities, and mentoring programs. The Hub aims to empower young people, helping them develop essential life skills and achieve their full potential.
    - **"Arsenal in the Community":** This program delivers a range of initiatives, including football coaching, educational workshops, and health and wellbeing programs, to engage with local communities and promote social inclusion.
    - **Supporting Disability Sports:** Arsenal is committed to promoting disability sports and providing opportunities for people with disabilities to participate in physical activity. The club's Disability Football program offers coaching and competitive opportunities for people of all ages and abilities.
- **Global Outreach:** Extending a Helping Hand Worldwide: The Foundation also supports international initiatives, partnering with organizations like Save the Children to deliver aid and support to vulnerable communities around the world.

    - **Save the Children Partnership:** Arsenal has a long-standing partnership with Save the Children, supporting various initiatives, including emergency relief efforts, education programs, and campaigns to protect children's rights.

- **Coaching for Life:** This program, run in partnership with Save the Children, uses football as a tool to support the physical and mental wellbeing of children in Jordan and Indonesia, providing them with valuable life skills and opportunities.

Arsenal's Values: A Guiding Framework

Underlying Arsenal's identity and culture is a set of core values that guide the club's actions and decisions. These values, deeply ingrained in the club's DNA, shape its interactions with players, staff, supporters, and the wider community.

- **Respect:** Arsenal promotes a culture of respect, valuing diversity and treating everyone with dignity and fairness. The club actively combats discrimination and promotes equality, fostering an inclusive environment for all, regardless of background, ethnicity, gender, or sexual orientation.
- **Excellence:** Arsenal strives for excellence in all aspects of its operations, from player performance to community engagement. The club is committed to continuous improvement and innovation, always seeking to push boundaries and achieve the highest standards, both on and off the pitch.
- **Community:** Arsenal recognizes the importance of its role in the local community and actively engages with its supporters and neighbors. The club's community programs and charitable initiatives demonstrate its commitment to making a positive impact beyond the football pitch, contributing to the social and economic wellbeing of the local area.

Conclusion:

Arsenal Football Club's identity is a complex and multifaceted tapestry, woven from tradition, innovation, and a deep commitment to community engagement. The club's iconic symbols, rituals, and values create a sense of belonging and shared identity for millions of fans worldwide. From the hallowed turf of Highbury to the modern marvel of the Emirates Stadium, Arsenal's physical spaces have become synonymous with the club's history and ambition. The club's legacy of innovation, both on and off the pitch, has kept it at the forefront of the game, while its commitment to social impact and community engagement has made a positive difference in the lives of many. As Arsenal continues to evolve and compete on the world stage, its identity and culture will remain a guiding force, shaping its actions and inspiring its supporters for generations to come.

Notebook Prompt: Use this space to jot down any new facts about football you learned from this section or ideas to share with other fans. You can also jot down any questions you have about these rules or how they apply in different game situations.

....

....

....

....

....

....

....

....

....

....

....

....

....

....

....

....

PART 2

LEGENDARY ARSENAL PLAYERS

CHAPTER 4

Player Profiles

Arsenal Legends: Profiles of Six Iconic Players

Arsenal Football Club boasts a rich history adorned with legendary figures who have etched their names into the club's folklore. This document provides detailed profiles of six such icons: Thierry Henry, Tony Adams, Dennis Bergkamp, Ian Wright, Patrick Vieira, and Cesc Fàbregas. Each player, in their unique way, has contributed significantly to Arsenal's success and left an indelible mark on the club's identity.

Thierry Henry (1999-2007, 2012): The King of Highbury

Thierry Henry, arguably the greatest player to ever don the Arsenal shirt, redefined the role of a striker with his breathtaking pace, clinical finishing, and unparalleled elegance.

- **Career Highlights:**
    - Arsenal's all-time leading goalscorer with 228 goals in all competitions.
    - Two Premier League titles (2002, 2004), including the Invincibles season.
    - Three FA Cups (2002, 2003, 2005).
    - Two-time PFA Players' Player of the Year (2003, 2004).

- Four-time Premier League Golden Boot winner.
- UEFA Champions League runner-up (2006).

- **Key Achievements:**
  - Transformed Arsenal's attack with his pace, power, and clinical finishing.
  - Led the Invincibles to an unbeaten Premier League season in 2003-04.
  - Scored some of the most memorable goals in Premier League history.

- **Memorable Moments:**
  - His iconic goal against Tottenham Hotspur in 2002, where he ran the length of the pitch before slotting the ball past the keeper.
  - His volley against Manchester United in 2000, a goal that epitomized his technical brilliance and athleticism.
  - His return to Arsenal in 2012, where he scored a dramatic winner against Leeds United in the FA Cup.

- **Unique Contributions:**
  - Elevated Arsenal to new heights with his goalscoring exploits and inspired performances.
  - Became a global icon and ambassador for the club.
  - His statue outside the Emirates Stadium immortalizes his legacy as a true Arsenal legend.

Tony Adams (1983-2002): Mr. Arsenal

Tony Adams, a one-club man and the epitome of leadership, captained Arsenal through a period of unprecedented success, embodying the club's values of resilience, determination, and unwavering commitment.

- **Career Highlights:**
  - Four league titles (1989, 1991, 1998, 2002).
  - Three FA Cups (1993, 1998, 2002).
  - Two League Cups (1987, 1993).
  - UEFA Cup Winners' Cup (1994).
- **Key Achievements:**
  - Formed a formidable defensive partnership with Steve Bould and Martin Keown.
  - Captained Arsenal to numerous trophies, including the Premier League and FA Cup double in 1998 and 2002.
  - Overcame personal challenges to become a role model for perseverance and dedication.
- **Memorable Moments:**
  - His iconic goal against Everton in 1998, which sealed the Premier League title.
  - His leadership during the 1990-91 season, where Arsenal lost only one league game.
  - His testimonial match in 2002, a testament to his enduring legacy at the club.
- **Unique Contributions:**
  - Embodied the spirit of Arsenal with his unwavering commitment and leadership.

    - His statue outside the Emirates Stadium recognizes his status as a true club legend.
    - Inspired a generation of young players with his dedication and professionalism.

Dennis Bergkamp (1995-2006): The Non-Flying Dutchman

Dennis Bergkamp, a master of technique and vision, revolutionized Arsenal's attack with his sublime touch, exquisite passing, and unparalleled creativity.

- **Career Highlights:**
    - Three Premier League titles (1998, 2002, 2004).
    - Four FA Cups (1998, 2002, 2003, 2005).
- **Key Achievements:**
    - Formed a formidable partnership with Thierry Henry, creating one of the most potent attacking duos in Premier League history.
    - Scored some of the most iconic goals in Arsenal's history, including his wonder goal against Newcastle United in 2002.
    - His vision and creativity transformed Arsenal's attacking style.
- **Memorable Moments:**
    - His hat-trick against Leicester City in 1997, showcasing his all-round ability.
    - His iconic goal against Newcastle United in 2002, a masterpiece of skill and improvisation.
    - His final game at Highbury in 2006, an emotional farewell to a true Arsenal legend.

- **Unique Contributions:**
    - Elevated Arsenal's attacking play with his artistry and creativity.
    - Inspired a generation of young players with his technical brilliance.
    - His statue outside the Emirates Stadium celebrates his legacy as one of the greatest players to ever grace the Premier League.

Ian Wright (1991-1998): The Goal Machine

Ian Wright, a prolific goalscorer and fan favorite, brought passion, energy, and a infectious enthusiasm to Arsenal, becoming a club legend with his record-breaking goalscoring exploits.

- **Career Highlights:**
    - Premier League title (1998).
    - FA Cup (1993).
    - League Cup (1993).
    - UEFA Cup Winners' Cup (1994).
- **Key Achievements:**
    - Broke Cliff Bastin's long-standing goalscoring record to become Arsenal's all-time leading scorer (a record later surpassed by Thierry Henry).
    - Scored 185 goals in 288 appearances for Arsenal.
    - His passionate celebrations and infectious enthusiasm endeared him to the fans.
- **Memorable Moments:**
    - His hat-trick against Southampton in 1997, which broke Bastin's record.
    - His winning goal against Sheffield Wednesday in the

1993 FA Cup final replay.
  - His emotional farewell to Highbury in 1998.
- **Unique Contributions:**
  - Brought a new dimension to Arsenal's attack with his pace, power, and clinical finishing.
  - His connection with the fans created a special bond between the team and its supporters.
  - His legacy as a goalscoring legend and a true Arsenal icon lives on.

Patrick Vieira (1996-2005): The Driving Force

Patrick Vieira, a powerful and dominant midfielder, was the driving force behind Arsenal's success in the late 1990s and early 2000s, leading the team with his strength, athleticism, and unwavering determination.

- **Career Highlights:**
  - Three Premier League titles (1998, 2002, 2004).
  - Four FA Cups (1998, 2002, 2003, 2005).
- **Key Achievements:**
  - Formed a formidable midfield partnership with Emmanuel Petit and Gilberto Silva.
  - Captained Arsenal to the Invincibles season in 2003-04.
  - His leadership and competitive spirit inspired his teammates.
- **Memorable Moments:**
  - His dominant performances in midfield battles against Manchester United's Roy Keane.
  - His crucial goal against Tottenham Hotspur in the

2001 FA Cup semi-final.
    - His emotional farewell to Highbury in 2005.
- **Unique Contributions:**
    - Provided the steel and dynamism that underpinned Arsenal's success.
    - His leadership and presence inspired his teammates and intimidated opponents.
    - His legacy as a dominant midfielder and a true Arsenal captain lives on.

Cesc Fàbregas (2003-2011): The Prodigy

Cesc Fàbregas, a precocious talent and a product of Arsenal's youth academy, emerged as a midfield maestro, captivating fans with his vision, passing range, and technical brilliance.

- **Career Highlights:**
    - FA Cup (2005).
    - UEFA Champions League runner-up (2006).
- **Key Achievements:**
    - Became Arsenal's youngest ever player and goalscorer.
    - Orchestrated Arsenal's attack with his vision, passing range, and creativity.
    - Captained the team at a young age, demonstrating his leadership qualities.
- **Memorable Moments:**
    - His dominant performance against Juventus in the 2006 Champions League quarter-final.
    - His long-range goal against Tottenham Hotspur in 2009.

- His emotional return to the Emirates Stadium with Chelsea in 2014.

- **Unique Contributions:**
    - Represented the success of Arsenal's youth development program.
    - His creativity and vision added a new dimension to Arsenal's midfield.
    - His legacy as a talented playmaker and a symbol of Arsenal's commitment to youth development endures.

These six players, each with their unique talents and contributions, have left an indelible mark on Arsenal Football Club. Their achievements, memorable moments, and lasting legacies have shaped the club's identity and inspired generations of fans. They are true Arsenal legends, forever etched in the hearts of Gooners worldwide.

Notebook Prompt: Use this space to jot down any new facts about football you learned from this section or ideas to share with other fans. You can also jot down any questions you have about these rules or how they apply in different game situations.

....

....

....

....

....

....

....

....

....

....

....

....

....

....

....

....

CHAPTER 5

Honorable Mentions

Beyond the Starting XI: A Deeper Dive into Arsenal's Supporting Cast

While the spotlight often shines brightest on the leading figures, Arsenal's history is enriched by a supporting cast of iconic players who played pivotal roles in the club's success. This expanded summary delves deeper into the contributions and memorable moments of four such players – Robert Pirès, Sol Campbell, Freddie Ljungberg, and Aaron Ramsey – providing a richer understanding of their impact on Arsenal's legacy.

Robert Pirès (2000-2006): The Wing Wizard

Robert Pirès, the epitome of Gallic flair and finesse, was more than just a winger; he was an artist on the pitch, weaving his magic down the left flank and creating a symphony of attacking movement with his mesmerizing dribbling skills, pinpoint crosses, and an almost telepathic understanding with Thierry Henry.

- **Significant Contributions:**
    - **Attacking Prowess:** Pirès's ability to glide past defenders with his effortless dribbling and deliver precise crosses made him a constant threat on the left wing. He formed a devastating partnership with Henry, their interplay and understanding creating numerous goals for the prolific striker. Pirès's vision

and ability to pick out a pass often unlocked defenses, creating scoring opportunities for himself and his teammates.

  - **Crucial Goals:** Pirès had a knack for scoring vital goals for Arsenal, often in crucial moments. His composure and clinical finishing in high-pressure situations made him a valuable asset. His winning goal in the 2003 FA Cup final against Southampton is a testament to his ability to deliver when it mattered most.
  - **Invincibles Season:** Pirès played a pivotal role in Arsenal's unbeaten 2003-04 Premier League campaign, contributing with goals and assists as the team made history. His consistency and creativity were essential to Arsenal's fluid attacking style, which saw them dismantle opponents with breathtaking football.

- **Memorable Moments:**

  - **FA Cup Final Winner (2003):** His decisive goal against Southampton in the 2003 FA Cup final, a calm finish after a mazy run, secured the trophy for Arsenal and etched his name in the club's history. This goal epitomized his ability to create something out of nothing and deliver in crucial moments.
  - **Premier League Title (2004):** Pirès was an integral part of the Invincibles squad, showcasing his consistency and creativity throughout the season. His understanding with Henry and his ability to unlock defenses were crucial to Arsenal's dominance in the league.
  - **Penalty Miss in the Champions League Final**

(2006): Despite missing a penalty in the 2006 Champions League final against Barcelona, Pirès's overall contribution to Arsenal's European campaign was significant. He played a key role in helping the team reach the final, showcasing his ability to perform on the biggest stage.

Sol Campbell (2001-2006, 2010): The Defensive Colossus

Sol Campbell, a towering figure in Arsenal's defense, arrived from Tottenham Hotspur in a controversial but ultimately impactful transfer. His strength, aerial dominance, and leadership qualities solidified Arsenal's backline and contributed to a period of sustained success.

- **Significant Contributions:**
    - **Defensive Solidity:** Campbell formed a formidable partnership with Kolo Touré, providing a rock-solid foundation for Arsenal's defense. His physical presence, tactical awareness, and ability to read the game made him a nightmare for opposing strikers. Campbell's dominance in the air was particularly impressive, making him a threat from set pieces and a reassuring presence in defense.
    - **Invincibles Season:** Campbell played every minute of Arsenal's unbeaten 2003-04 Premier League season, a testament to his consistency and importance to the team's success. His ability to marshal the defense and nullify opposing threats was crucial to Arsenal's historic achievement.
    - **Leadership Qualities:** Campbell's leadership and experience were invaluable to Arsenal, especially

during crucial matches and high-pressure situations. His vocal presence on the pitch and his ability to organize the defense instilled confidence in his teammates and helped maintain a calm and composed approach.

- **Memorable Moments:**
  - **Champions League Goal (2006):** His towering header in the 2006 Champions League final against Barcelona gave Arsenal the lead and highlighted his aerial prowess. This goal, though ultimately not enough to secure victory, showcased Campbell's ability to contribute at both ends of the pitch.
  - **Invincibles Season (2003-04):** Campbell's unwavering defensive displays throughout the Invincibles season were crucial to the team's historic achievement. His ability to keep clean sheets and provide a solid foundation for the attack was a key factor in Arsenal's unbeaten run.
  - **North London Derby Dominance:** His performances in North London derbies against his former club, Tottenham, were often characterized by passion and determination. Campbell relished the challenge of facing his old rivals, and his performances in these high-stakes matches were often inspirational.

Freddie Ljungberg (1998-2007): The Stylish Swede

Freddie Ljungberg, the versatile and stylish midfielder, was a key figure in Arsenal's attacking lineup during the late 1990s and early 2000s. His flair, goalscoring ability, and iconic red hair made him a fan favorite and a symbol of Arsenal's attacking prowess.

- **Significant Contributions:**
  - **Attacking Versatility:** Ljungberg's ability to play on either wing or through the center made him a valuable asset to Wenger's squad. His pace, dribbling skills, and eye for goal provided an attacking spark from various positions. He was equally adept at cutting inside from the wing and delivering a shot or making incisive runs through the center to create scoring opportunities.
  - **Crucial Goals:** Ljungberg had a knack for scoring important goals for Arsenal, often arriving in the box at the right time to finish off attacking moves. His goal in the 2002 FA Cup final against Chelsea is a prime example of his ability to deliver in crucial moments.
  - **Invincibles Season:** Ljungberg played a significant role in the Invincibles season, contributing with goals and assists as Arsenal achieved the unthinkable. His ability to link up with Henry and Bergkamp in attack and his tireless running made him an integral part of the team's success.

- **Memorable Moments:**
  - **FA Cup Final Goal (2002):** His stunning solo goal against Chelsea in the 2002 FA Cup final, where he dribbled past several defenders before slotting the ball past Carlo Cudicini, sealed the victory for Arsenal and showcased his individual brilliance. This goal is often replayed as one of the greatest in FA Cup final history.
  - **Premier League Title (2004):** Ljungberg was a key member of the Invincibles squad, demonstrating his

versatility and attacking threat throughout the season. His ability to adapt to different roles and contribute consistently made him a valuable asset to the team.

  - **Iconic Red Hair:** His distinctive red hair became synonymous with Arsenal's success during his time at the club, making him a recognizable figure both on and off the pitch. His hairstyle, along with his stylish play, made him a cult hero among Arsenal fans.

Aaron Ramsey (2008-2019): The Welsh Dragon

Aaron Ramsey, the dynamic and box-to-box midfielder, joined Arsenal as a promising youngster and developed into a key player for the club. His energy, tenacity, and knack for scoring crucial goals endeared him to the Arsenal faithful.

- **Significant Contributions:**
  - **Box-to-Box Dynamism:** Ramsey's energy, work rate, and ability to contribute both defensively and offensively made him a valuable asset in Arsenal's midfield. He was a tireless runner, covering every blade of grass and making crucial interceptions and tackles. His ability to drive forward with the ball and make late runs into the box made him a constant threat in attack.
  - **FA Cup Hero:** Ramsey scored winning goals in two FA Cup finals (2014 and 2017), etching his name in Arsenal's cup history. His ability to deliver in crucial moments, scoring decisive goals in high-pressure matches, made him a fan favorite and earned him the reputation of a "big-game player."
  - **Leadership and Commitment:** Ramsey's dedication to the club and his willingness to fight for the badge

earned him the respect of his teammates and supporters. He was a passionate and committed player who always gave his all for the team, even during difficult periods.

- **Memorable Moments:**
    - **FA Cup Winning Goals (2014, 2017):** His decisive goals in the 2014 and 2017 FA Cup finals against Hull City and Chelsea, respectively, secured the trophy for Arsenal and cemented his status as a cup hero. These goals, scored with composure and precision, demonstrated his ability to rise to the occasion and deliver when it mattered most.
    - **Goal against Galatasaray (2014):** His stunning volley against Galatasaray in the Champions League, struck with power and accuracy, showcased his technical ability and earned him widespread acclaim. This goal is often replayed as one of the greatest goals in Champions League history.
    - **Emotional Farewell (2019):** His emotional farewell to the Emirates Stadium in 2019, after 11 years of service to the club, highlighted his connection with the fans and his contribution to Arsenal. The outpouring of support from the fans demonstrated the deep affection they held for Ramsey and his dedication to the club.

These four players, along with countless others, have contributed to the rich tapestry of Arsenal's history. Their significant contributions, memorable moments, and unique qualities have enriched the club's legacy and inspired generations of fans. They represent the diverse talent and unwavering spirit that have defined Arsenal Football Club throughout its illustrious history.

Notebook Prompt: Use this space to jot down any new facts about football you learned from this section or ideas to share with other fans. You can also jot down any questions you have about these rules or how they apply in different game situations.

………………………………………………………………………………

………………………………………………………………………………

………………………………………………………………………………

………………………………………………………………………………

………………………………………………………………………………

………………………………………………………………………………

………………………………………………………………………………

………………………………………………………………………………

………………………………………………………………………………

………………………………………………………………………………

………………………………………………………………………………

………………………………………………………………………………

………………………………………………………………………………

………………………………………………………………………………

………………………………………………………………………………

………………………………………………………………………………

PART 3

ARSENAL TRIVIA AND FUN GAMES

CHAPTER 6

True or False Questions

1. Arsenal FC was founded in 1886.
2. The club's original name was Dial Square.
3. Arsenal's home ground is called Old Trafford.
4. Herbert Chapman managed Arsenal in the 1930s.
5. Arsenal won the league and cup double in the 1970-71 season.
6. George Graham managed Arsenal to the Cup Winners' Cup in 1994.
7. Arsene Wenger became Arsenal manager in 1996.
8. The Invincibles went an entire Premier League season unbeaten in 2004-05.
9. Thierry Henry is Arsenal's all-time top goalscorer.
10. Arsenal have won the FA Cup a record 14 times.
11. The club's nickname is the Gunners.
12. Arsenal's traditional home kit is red and white.
13. The club moved to Emirates Stadium in 2006.
14. Arsenal won the Premier League title in the 2015-16 season.
15. Tony Adams captained the Invincibles.
16. Ian Wright scored over 100 goals for Arsenal.
17. Dennis Bergkamp wore the number 10 shirt for Arsenal.
18. Patrick Vieira was a key part of Arsenal's midfield in the late 1990s and early 2000s.
19. Arsenal have never been relegated from the top flight of English football.
20. The North London Derby is contested between Arsenal and Tottenham Hotspur.
21. Arsenal beat Liverpool on penalties to win the 1987 League Cup final.
22. The club's motto is "Victoria Concordia Crescit" which means

"Victory Through Harmony".

23. Arsenal Women have won the Women's Super League title.
24. The Clock End was a famous stand at Arsenal's former ground, Highbury.
25. David Seaman was Arsenal's goalkeeper in the 1990s and early 2000s.
26. Freddie Ljungberg was known for his distinctive red hair.
27. Robert Pires was part of the Invincibles team.
28. Sol Campbell joined Arsenal from Tottenham Hotspur.
29. Cesc Fabregas was a product of Arsenal's youth academy.
30. Robin van Persie left Arsenal to join Manchester City.
31. Theo Walcott was known for his blistering pace.
32. Andrey Arshavin scored four goals in one game against Liverpool at Anfield.
33. Nicklas Bendtner claimed he was one of the best strikers in the world.
34. Bacary Sagna played right-back for Arsenal.
35. Arsenal hold the record for the longest unbeaten run in English football history.
36. The FA Cup final is traditionally held at Wembley Stadium.
37. Arsenal have won the League Cup three times.
38. The Community Shield is contested between the winners of the Premier League and the FA Cup.
39. Arsenal reached the Champions League final in 2006.
40. The club has a strong rivalry with Manchester United.
41. Ken Friar has held various roles at Arsenal for over 70 years.
42. Arsenal Ladies were formed in 1987.
43. The club has a statue of Herbert Chapman outside Emirates Stadium.
44. Arsenal's first ever game was a 6-0 win.
45. The club has had a shirt sponsorship deal with Adidas.
46. Arsenal were the first club to wear numbered shirts in a league match.
47. The club has toured internationally to play friendly matches.
48. Arsenal have a youth academy that has produced many talented players.
49. The club has been involved in community projects and initiatives.
50. Arsenal shares its name with a Russian football club.

51. Arsenal once played a match in a blizzard against Dynamo Moscow.
52. The club has a mascot named Gunnersaurus Rex.
53. Arsenal Women's team play their home games at Meadow Park.
54. The club has been featured in films and television shows.
55. Arsenal has a large global fanbase.
56. The club has a museum dedicated to its history.
57. Arsenal has had players from many different countries.
58. The club has been involved in various charitable activities.
59. Arsenal has a strong online presence with millions of followers on social media.
60. The club has released official merchandise such as clothing, accessories, and memorabilia.
61. Arsenal has a training ground called London Colney.
62. The club has had players who have won the Ballon d'Or award.
63. Arsenal has a supporters' trust that represents the interests of fans.
64. The club has been involved in initiatives to promote equality and diversity.
65. Arsenal has a dedicated fanzine culture.
66. The club has a history of producing homegrown talent through its academy.
67. Arsenal has been involved in partnerships with other football clubs around the world.
68. The club has a board of directors that oversees its operations.
69. Arsenal has been the subject of books and documentaries.
70. The club has a strong connection with the local community in North London.
71. Sylvain Wiltord scored the winning goal in the 2002 FA Cup Final against Chelsea.
72. Nwankwo Kanu scored a hat-trick against Chelsea after coming off the bench.
73. Arsenal won the FA Cup in 1979 with a last-minute goal from Alan Sunderland.
74. Charlie George scored a spectacular volley in the 1971 FA Cup Final.
75. Paul Merson was known for his struggles with addiction.
76. David Rocastle was a popular player with the fans in the late 1980s and early 1990s.

77. Martin Keown was known for his passionate celebrations.
78. Lee Dixon was a reliable right-back for Arsenal for many years.
79. Nigel Winterburn was a consistent left-back for Arsenal in the 1990s.
80. Steve Bould was a solid central defender alongside Tony Adams.
81. Ray Parlour was nicknamed "The Romford Pele".
82. Emmanuel Petit scored the third goal in the 1998 World Cup Final for France.
83. Marc Overmars was a skillful winger for Arsenal in the late 1990s.
84. Arsenal beat Sheffield Wednesday on penalties in the 1993 FA Cup Final replay.
85. Gilles Grimandi was a versatile player who could play in defense or midfield.
86. Nelson Vivas was an Argentinian defender who played for Arsenal in the late 1990s.
87. Kolo Toure was an Ivorian defender who formed a strong partnership with Sol Campbell.
88. Lauren was a Cameroonian right-back who was part of the Invincibles team.
89. Jens Lehmann was known for his eccentric personality.
90. Gilberto Silva was a Brazilian defensive midfielder who provided stability to the team.
91. Edu was a Brazilian midfielder who was a popular figure at Arsenal.
92. Jose Antonio Reyes was a Spanish winger who joined Arsenal for a then club-record fee.
93. Mathieu Flamini was a French midfielder known for his energetic performances.
94. Alexander Hleb was a Belarusian midfielder who was known for his dribbling skills.
95. Emmanuel Adebayor was a Togolese striker who scored many goals for Arsenal.
96. Gael Clichy was a French left-back who came through the Arsenal academy.
97. Philippe Senderos was a Swiss defender who was prone to the occasional mistake.
98. Johan Djourou was a Swiss defender who spent many years at

Arsenal.

99. Tomas Rosicky was a Czech midfielder who was often injured during his time at Arsenal.
100. Abou Diaby was a French midfielder who suffered from many injury problems.
101. Carlos Vela was a Mexican forward who showed glimpses of his talent at Arsenal.
102. Nicklas Bendtner scored a late winner against Tottenham Hotspur in the 2007 North London Derby.
103. Arsenal women's team has won the FA Cup more times than any other team.
104. Arsenal holds the record for the most consecutive clean sheets in the Premier League.
105. Arsenal has a partnership with a Rwandan football club.
106. The club has been criticized for its ticket prices.
107. Arsenal has a large following in Asia.
108. The club has been involved in initiatives to promote sustainability.
109. Arsenal has a dedicated app for fans.
110. The club has a history of signing French players.
111. Arsenal once wore a bruised banana kit.
112. The club has been accused of lacking ambition in the transfer market.
113. Arsenal has a good record against teams from the north of England.
114. The club has a reputation for playing attractive football.
115. Arsenal has been involved in some controversial matches with Manchester United.
116. The club has a strong scouting network.
117. Arsenal has been praised for its youth development program.
118. The club has a good relationship with its former players.
119. Arsenal has been involved in some memorable European nights at Highbury.
120. The club has a strong commercial presence.
121. Arsenal has a history of signing players from South America.
122. The club has been involved in some thrilling comebacks in matches.
123. Arsenal has a reputation for being a well-run club.
124. The club has a loyal fanbase.

125. Arsenal has been involved in some dramatic penalty shootouts.
126. The club has a history of producing players for the England national team.
127. Arsenal has a strong rivalry with Chelsea.
128. The club has been involved in some memorable FA Cup finals.
129. Arsenal has a reputation for being a stylish club.
130. The club has a strong connection with the city of London.
131. Highbury had a capacity of over 60,000.
132. Arsenal's first game at Emirates Stadium was against Ajax.
133. The Emirates Stadium has a statue of Dennis Bergkamp outside.
134. Arsenal shares the Emirates Stadium with another football club.
135. The stadium has hosted music concerts.
136. The stadium has retractable roof.
137. The stadium has a club shop selling merchandise.
138. The stadium has a capacity of over 100,000.
139. The stadium is located in Islington.
140. The stadium has hosted international football matches.
141. The name "Arsenal" was chosen because the founders worked in the Royal Arsenal armament factory.
142. Arsenal's first trophy was the London Charity Cup in 1891.
143. The club was invited to join the Football League First Division in 1919 despite finishing fifth in the Second Division the previous season.
144. Arsenal has had more than 20 different managers throughout its history.
145. The club's colors were originally redcurrant and white.
146. Arsenal women's team is the most successful team in English women's football history.
147. The club has a partnership with Puma for its kit manufacturing.
148. Arsenal has a dedicated TV channel called Arsenal TV.
149. The club has a large following in Africa.
150. Arsenal has a strong commitment to developing young players.
151. Arsenal has a higher average attendance than Tottenham

Hotspur.

152. The club has won the Inter-Cities Fairs Cup.
153. Arsenal has never won the European Cup/Champions League.
154. The club has a strong record in the FA Youth Cup.
155. Arsenal has a training ground in Hertfordshire.
156. The club has a partnership with Emirates Airline.
157. Arsenal has a large number of supporters' clubs around the world.
158. The club has a dedicated foundation that supports charitable causes.
159. Arsenal has a history of signing players from the Netherlands.
160. The club has been involved in some memorable matches against Barcelona.
161. Arsenal has a reputation for developing young players who go on to have successful careers elsewhere.
162. The club has a strong social media presence.
163. Arsenal has a history of signing players from Germany.
164. The club has been involved in some memorable matches against Bayern Munich.
165. Arsenal has a reputation for being a forward-thinking club.
166. The club has a strong commitment to community engagement.
167. Arsenal has a history of signing players from Spain.
168. The club has been involved in some memorable matches against Real Madrid.
169. Arsenal has a reputation for being a well-respected club.
170. The club has a strong commitment to fan engagement.
171. Arsenal Women have won the Continental Cup (League Cup).
172. Arsenal have been managed by a Scotsman, a Frenchman, and a Spaniard.
173. Liam Brady was a famous Irish player for Arsenal in the 1970s.
174. Arsenal were the first team to win the FA Cup at the new Wembley Stadium in 2000.
175. The club has a partnership with Adidas for its kit manufacturing.
176. Arsenal has a dedicated radio station called Arsenal Player.

177. The club has a large following in North America.
178. Arsenal has a strong commitment to financial fair play.
179. Arsenal's away kit has traditionally been yellow and blue.
180. The club has been involved in some memorable matches against Liverpool.
181. Arsenal has a reputation for being a club that plays attacking football.
182. The club has a strong commitment to developing its youth academy.
183. Arsenal has a history of signing players from Africa.
184. The club has been involved in some memorable matches against Chelsea in the Champions League.
185. Arsenal has a reputation for being a club that is open to new ideas.
186. The club has a strong commitment to its values.
187. Arsenal has a history of signing players from Eastern Europe.
188. The club has been involved in some memorable matches against Manchester City in recent years.
189. Arsenal has a reputation for being a club that is difficult to beat at home.
190. The club has a strong commitment to its staff.
191. Perry Groves won two league titles with Arsenal.
192. Alan Smith was top scorer in the 1990-91 title-winning season.
193. David O'Leary holds the record for the most appearances for Arsenal.
194. The club's anthem is "God Save the Queen".
195. Arsenal has a statue of Tony Adams outside the Emirates Stadium.
196. The club was the subject of a fly-on-the-wall documentary series called "Arsenal: All or Nothing".
197. Arsenal has a partnership with Gatorade.
198. The club has a large following in Australia.
199. Arsenal has a strong commitment to player welfare.
200. Arsenal's current manager is Mikel Arteta.

Answer Key

1. True	101. True
2. True	102. True
3. False	103. True
4. True	104. True
5. True	105. True
6. True	106. True
7. True	107. True
8. True	108. True
9. True	109. True
10. True	110. True
11. True	111. True
12. True	112. True
13. True	113. False
14. False	114. True
15. False	115. True
16. True	116. True
17. True	117. True
18. True	118. True
19. False	119. True
20. True	120. True
21. True	121. True
22. True	122. True
23. True	123. True
24. True	124. True
25. True	125. True
26. True	126. True
27. True	127. True
28. True	128. False
29. True	129. True
30. False	130. False
31. True	131. True
32. True	132. False
33. True	133. True
34. True	134. False
35. True	135. True
36. True	136. False
37. False	137. True
38. True	138. True

39. True	139. True
40. True	140. True
41. True	141. True
42. True	142. True
43. True	143. False
44. True	144. False
45. True	145. True
46. True	146. True
47. True	147. True
48. True	148. True
49. True	149. True
50. True	150. True
51. True	151. True
52. True	152. True
53. True	153. True
54. True	154. True
55. True	155. True
56. True	156. True
57. True	157. True
58. True	158. True
59. True	159. True
60. True	160. True
61. True	161. True
62. True	162. True
63. True	163. True
64. True	164. True
65. True	165. True
66. True	166. True
67. True	167. True
68. True	168. True
69. True	169. True
70. True	170. True
71. True	171. False
72. True	172. True
73. True	173. True
74. True	174. False
75. True	175. True
76. True	176. True

77. True 78. True 79. True 80. True 81. True 82. True 83. True 84. True 85. True 86. True 87. True 88. True 89. True 90. True 91. True 92. True 93. True 94. True 95. True 96. True 97. True 98. True 99. True 100. True	177. True 178. True 179. True 180. True 181. True 182. True 183. True 184. True 185. True 186. True 187. True 188. True 189. True 190. True 191. True 192. True 193. True 194. False 195. True 196. True 197. True 198. True 199. True 200. True

Notebook Prompt: Use this space to jot down any new facts about football you learned from this section or ideas to share with other fans. You can also jot down any questions you have about these rules or how they apply in different game situations.

....

....

....

....

....

....

....

....

....

....

....

....

....

....

....

....

CHAPTER 7

Arsenal Knowledge Quiz

History

1. When was Arsenal FC founded?
2. What was the club's original name?
3. In what year did Arsenal join the Football League?
4. When did Arsenal first win the FA Cup?
5. Who was Arsenal's manager during their dominant period in the 1930s?
6. In what year did Arsenal win their first league and cup double?
7. Who managed Arsenal to the Cup Winners' Cup in 1994?
8. When did Arsene Wenger become Arsenal manager?
9. In what season did Arsenal go an entire Premier League season unbeaten?
10. When did Arsenal move to Emirates Stadium?
11. What is the name of Arsenal's former stadium?
12. What year did Arsenal win the league title under George Graham?
13. When did Arsenal win their last League Cup?
14. How many times have Arsenal won the FA Cup?
15. What is Arsenal's highest ever league finish?

16. Who were the opponents in the 1987 League Cup final?

17. When did Arsenal win their first European trophy?

18. What is the meaning of Arsenal's motto, "Victoria Concordia Crescit"?

19. When were Arsenal Ladies (now Arsenal Women) formed?

20. Who scored the winning goal for Arsenal in the 2002 FA Cup Final?

Players

21. Who is Arsenal's all-time top goalscorer?

22. Which player holds the record for the most appearances for Arsenal?

23. Who scored Arsenal's fastest ever Premier League goal?

24. Which player scored a hat-trick against Chelsea after coming off the bench?

25. Who scored the winning goal in the 1979 FA Cup Final?

26. Who scored a spectacular volley in the 1971 FA Cup Final?

27. Which Arsenal player was nicknamed "The Romford Pele"?

28. Which Arsenal player scored the third goal in the 1998 World Cup Final for France?

29. Which Arsenal player scored four goals in one game against Liverpool at Anfield?

30. Which former Arsenal captain is known for his struggles with addiction?

31. Which Arsenal player was known for his passionate celebrations?

32. Which Arsenal player was known for his eccentric personality?

33. Which Arsenal player claimed he was one of the best strikers in the world?

34. Which Arsenal player was a popular figure with the fans in the late 1980s and early 1990s?

35. Which Arsenal player was known for his distinctive red hair?

36. Which Arsenal player joined Arsenal from Tottenham Hotspur?

37. Which Arsenal player was a product of Arsenal's youth academy and later became captain?

38. Which Arsenal player left Arsenal to join Manchester United?

39. Which Arsenal player was known for his blistering pace?

40. Which Arsenal player was a skillful winger for Arsenal in the late 1990s?

Stadium Trivia

41. What is the capacity of Emirates Stadium?

42. What was the capacity of Highbury Stadium?

43. What year did Arsenal move into Highbury?

44. What is the name of the famous clock that used to be at Highbury?

45. Which stand at Emirates Stadium is known for housing the most vocal Arsenal supporters?

46. What is the name of the statue outside Emirates Stadium that commemorates a famous manager?

47. Which famous former player has a statue outside Emirates Stadium?

48. Has Emirates Stadium ever hosted an FA Cup Final?

49. What other events besides football matches have been held at Emirates Stadium?

50. What is the nearest London Underground station to Emirates Stadium?

Key Moments

51. In what year did Arsenal complete an unbeaten league season?

52. Which team did Arsenal beat in the 2005 FA Cup Final on penalties?

53. Who scored the winning penalty in that final?

54. Which team did Arsenal beat in the 1998 FA Cup Final to secure the Double?

55. Which team did Arsenal beat in the 1971 FA Cup Final to secure the Double?

56. In what year did Arsenal win the European Cup Winners' Cup?

57. Which team did they beat in the final?

58. What was the scoreline in the famous 4-4 draw with Tottenham Hotspur in 2008?

59. Who scored the winning goal for Arsenal in the 2014 FA Cup Final after extra time?

60. Who scored the equalizing goal for Arsenal in the 2017 FA Cup Final?

Managers

61. Who was Arsenal's longest-serving manager?

62. Which manager led Arsenal to the Double in 1971?

63. Which manager led Arsenal to the Double in 1998?

64. Which manager led Arsenal to the Invincibles season?

65. Who was the first manager to win a trophy at Emirates Stadium?

66. Which manager led Arsenal to three FA Cup titles in four years?

67. Which former Arsenal player is the current manager?

68. Which manager was in charge when Arsenal moved to Highbury?

69. Which manager signed Dennis Bergkamp?

70. Which manager was nicknamed "The Professor"?

Records

71. What is Arsenal's record win in the Premier League?

72. What is Arsenal's record defeat in the Premier League?

73. Who holds the record for the most goals scored in a single season for Arsenal?

74. What is the longest unbeaten run in Arsenal's history?

75. How many consecutive clean sheets did Arsenal keep in the 2003-04 season?

76. What is the highest attendance ever recorded at Highbury?

77. What is the highest attendance ever recorded at Emirates Stadium?

78. How many trophies did Arsene Wenger win as Arsenal manager?

79. How many times have Arsenal finished second in the Premier League?

80. What is the record number of goals scored by an Arsenal player in a single Premier League game?

Current Squad

81. Who is the current captain of Arsenal?

82. Which player wears the number 10 shirt for Arsenal?

83. Which Arsenal player is the current top scorer for the England national team?

84. Which current Arsenal player came through the Hale End academy?

85. Which current Arsenal player joined from Manchester City?

86. Which current Arsenal player is known for his impressive passing range?

87. Which current Arsenal player is known for his strong defensive abilities?

88. Which current Arsenal player is known for his pace and dribbling skills?

89. Which current Arsenal player is a left-footed attacking midfielder?

90. Who is Arsenal's current first-choice goalkeeper?

Youth Academy

91. What is the name of Arsenal's youth academy?

92. Which former Arsenal player is now a coach at the academy?

93. Which current Arsenal player graduated from the academy and won the Golden Boy award?

94. Which famous former Arsenal player came through the academy in the 1990s?

95. Which former academy graduate is now playing for Chelsea?

96. Which former academy graduate is now playing for Manchester City?

97. Which former academy graduate is now a manager?

98. How many FA Youth Cups has Arsenal won?

99. Which current England international came through the Arsenal academy?

100. Which former academy graduate is now a pundit?

Women's Team

101. Who is the current captain of Arsenal Women?

102. Who is the all-time leading goalscorer for Arsenal Women?

103. How many Women's Super League titles have Arsenal Women won?

104. How many FA Cups have Arsenal Women won?

105. Which Arsenal Women player has won the Ballon d'Or Féminin?

106. Which current Arsenal Women player represents the Netherlands national team?

107. Where do Arsenal Women play their home matches?

108. Who is the current manager of Arsenal Women?

109. In what year did Arsenal Women win their first league title?

110. Which trophy did Arsenal Women win in the 2018-19 season?

Club Culture

111. What is the name of Arsenal's club mascot?

112. What is the name of the popular Arsenal fan channel on YouTube?

113. What is the name of the Arsenal fanzine that has been running since 1989?

114. What is the name of the song that is traditionally sung by Arsenal fans before kick-off?

115. What is the nickname given to the rivalry between Arsenal and Tottenham Hotspur?

116. What is the name of the Arsenal supporters' trust?

117. What color is the away kit that Arsenal wore in the 1970s and is now considered iconic?

118. What food is traditionally sold outside Arsenal's stadiums?

119. Which celebrity is a well-known Arsenal fan?

120. What is the name of the club's official charity?

Club Legends

121. Who was known as "Mr. Arsenal"?

122. Which legendary Arsenal player wore the number 7 shirt?

123. Which former Arsenal captain is now a successful manager?

124. Which former Arsenal player is known for his punditry work on Sky Sports?

125. Which former Arsenal goalkeeper is considered one of the best in Premier League history?

126. Which former Arsenal player was known for his incredible technique and vision?

127. Which former Arsenal player was known for his powerful free kicks?

128. Which former Arsenal player was known for his leadership and defensive solidity?

129. Which former Arsenal player was known for his versatility and ability to play in multiple positions?

130. Which former Arsenal player was known for his acrobatic goal celebrations?

Memorable Matches

131. What was the scoreline in the 2006 Champions League Final between Arsenal and Barcelona?

132. Which team did Arsenal beat in the 1994 European Cup Winners' Cup Final?

133. What was the scoreline in the 2011 League Cup Final between Arsenal and Birmingham City?

134. In which year did Arsenal beat Manchester United 1-0 at Old Trafford with a goal from Marc Overmars?

135. Who scored the winning goal for Arsenal in the 2003 FA Cup Final against Southampton?

136. What was the scoreline in the 1989 First Division title decider between Arsenal and Liverpool at Anfield?

137. In which year did Arsenal beat Sheffield Wednesday on penalties in the FA Cup Final replay?

138. Which team did Arsenal beat in the 2015 FA Cup Final?

139. What was the scoreline in the 2004 Champions League quarter-final second leg between Arsenal and Chelsea?

140. Who scored the winning goal for Arsenal in the 1971 FA Cup Final against Liverpool?

Miscellaneous

141. How many times has Arsenal won the Community Shield?

142. What is the name of the Arsenal stadium tour?

143. What year did Arsenal adopt the cannon as its club crest?

144. Which London borough is Emirates Stadium located in?

145. What is the name of the Arsenal training ground?

146. Who is the current majority shareholder of Arsenal FC?

147. What is the name of the Arsenal fan group known for their vocal support and displays?

148. Which former Arsenal player has a stand named after him at Emirates Stadium?

149. What is the name of the documentary series about Arsenal released in 2022?

150. What social media platform did Arsenal join in 2008?

European Adventures

151. In which season did Arsenal reach the UEFA Cup Final?

152. Who scored Arsenal's goal in the 2006 Champions League Final?

153. Which team knocked Arsenal out of the Champions League in the Round of 16 in 2017?

154. How many times has Arsenal reached the semi-finals of the Champions League?

155. Which team did Arsenal beat in the 1994 European Cup Winners' Cup semi-final?

156. Which city hosted the 2000 UEFA Cup Final, which Arsenal lost on penalties?

157. In which season did Arsenal achieve their biggest ever Champions League win?

158. Who scored a hat-trick for Arsenal against Standard Liege in the 2009-10 Champions League group stage?

159. Which team did Arsenal beat in the 2019 Europa League semi-final?

160. Who was the manager when Arsenal last reached a European final?

Premier League Era

161. In which season did the Premier League first begin?

162. How many Premier League titles has Arsenal won?

163. Who was the first Arsenal player to score a Premier League hat-trick?

164. Which team did Arsenal beat 5-0 on the final day of the 2004-05 Premier League season?

165. Who scored the winning goal for Arsenal in the 2002

Premier League title decider against Manchester United at Old Trafford?

166. In which season did Arsenal finish second in the Premier League to Leicester City?

167. Which team did Arsenal beat 7-0 in the Premier League in 2013?

168. Who was the Premier League's top scorer in the 2011-12 season while playing for Arsenal?

169. Which current Premier League manager played for Arsenal in the 1990s?

170. Who was the manager when Arsenal last won the Premier League title?

Kits & Sponsors

171. What is the nickname given to Arsenal's yellow and blue away kit?

172. Which manufacturer currently produces Arsenal's kits?

173. Who was Arsenal's shirt sponsor between 1999 and 2006?

174. What color was the controversial away kit that Arsenal wore for one season in the mid-1990s?

175. In which decade did Arsenal first have a shirt sponsor?

176. Which company is Arsenal's current sleeve sponsor?

177. What color was the away kit that Arsenal wore when they won the double in 1998?

178. Which company was Arsenal's first ever shirt sponsor?

179. What is the name of the company that sponsors the Arsenal training ground?

180. What color was the third kit that Arsenal wore in the 2020-21 season?

Around the Club

181. What is the name of Arsenal's official charity foundation?

182. Who is the current chairman of Arsenal FC?

183. What is the name of the Arsenal museum?

184. Where can you find the Arsenal training ground?

185. What is the name of the club magazine published by Arsenal?

186. What year did Arsenal launch their official website?

187. What is the name of the Arsenal credit card?

188. Which airline is Arsenal's official airline partner?

189. What is the name of the official Arsenal app?

190. Who composed the current version of Arsenal's club anthem, "Victoria Concordia Crescit"?

Just for Fun

191. Which Arsenal player appeared in the film "The Inbetweeners Movie"?

192. Which former Arsenal player is known for his "Spiderman" celebration?

193. Which former Arsenal player released a rap single called "Gimme the Ball"?

194. Which Arsenal manager was famously hit by a pizza thrown by Sir Alex Ferguson?

195. Which former Arsenal player was nicknamed "Rocky"?

196. Which former Arsenal player is known for his catchphrase "She Wore a Yellow Ribbon"?

197. Which former Arsenal player is a qualified helicopter pilot?

198. Which former Arsenal player appeared on the reality TV

show "I'm a Celebrity...Get Me Out of Here!"?

199. Which former Arsenal player is married to a pop star?

200. Which former Arsenal player is known for his love of horses?

Answer Key

History
1. 1886
2. Dial Square
3. 1893
4. 1930
5. Herbert Chapman
6. 1971
7. George Graham
8. 1996
9. 2003-04
10. 2006
11. Highbury
12. 1991
13. 2011
14. 14
15. 1st
16. Liverpool
17. 1994 (European Cup Winners' Cup)
18. "Victory Through Harmony"
19. 1987
20. Sylvain Wiltord

Players

Women's Team
101. Kim Little
102. Kelly Smith
103. 3
104. 14
105. Vivianne Miedema (2021)
106. Vivianne Miedema
107. Meadow Park, Borehamwood
108. Jonas Eidevall
109. 1993
110. FA Women's League Cup

Club Culture
111. Gunnersaurus Rex
112. AFTV (Arsenal Fan TV)
113. The Gooner
114. "North London Forever"
115. The North London Derby
116. The Arsenal Supporters' Trust (AST)

21. Thierry Henry

22. David O'Leary

23. Kevin Campbell (10 seconds)

24. Nwankwo Kanu

25. Alan Sunderland

26. Charlie George

27. Ray Parlour

28. Emmanuel Petit

29. Andrey Arshavin

30. Paul Merson

31. Martin Keown

32. Jens Lehmann

33. Nicklas Bendtner

34. David Rocastle

35. Freddie Ljungberg

36. Sol Campbell

37. Cesc Fabregas

38. Robin van Persie (to Manchester United)

39. Theo Walcott

40. Marc Overmars

Stadium Trivia

41. Approximately 60,704

42. 38,419

43. 1913

44. The Clock End Clock

117. Bruised Banana

118. Pies

119. Piers Morgan (though many fans would prefer not to claim him!)

120. The Arsenal Foundation

Club Legends

121. Ken Friar

122. Robert Pires

123. Mikel Arteta

124. Paul Merson

125. David Seaman

126. Dennis Bergkamp

127. Thierry Henry

128. Tony Adams

129. Lee Dixon

130. Thierry Henry

Memorable Matches

131. Arsenal 1-2 Barcelona

132. Parma

133. Arsenal 1-2 Birmingham City

134. 1998

135. Robert Pires

136. Liverpool 0-2 Arsenal

137. 1993

45. The North Bank 46. Herbert Chapman 47. Dennis Bergkamp 48. No 49. Concerts, boxing matches, American football games 50. Arsenal station Key Moments 51. 2004 52. Manchester United 53. Patrick Vieira 54. Newcastle United 55. Liverpool 56. 1994 57. Parma 58. Arsenal 4-4 Tottenham Hotspur 59. Aaron Ramsey 60. Alexis Sanchez Managers 61. Arsene Wenger (1996-2018) 62. Bertie Mee 63. Arsene Wenger 64. Arsene Wenger 65. Arsene Wenger 66. Arsene Wenger 67. Mikel Arteta	138. Aston Villa 139. Arsenal 2-2 Chelsea (Arsenal won on away goals) 140. Charlie George Miscellaneous 141. 16 (shared record with Liverpool) 142. "Arsenal Museum and Stadium Tour" 143. 1949 144. Islington 145. London Colney 146. Stan Kroenke 147. The Ashburton Army 148. Ken Friar 149. "Arsenal: All or Nothing" 150. Facebook European Adventures 151. 2000 152. Sol Campbell 153. Bayern Munich 154. 2 (2006 and 2009) 155. Paris Saint-Germain 156. Copenhagen 157. 7-0 vs. Slavia Prague (2007-08 Champions League group stage)

68. Herbert Chapman

69. Bruce Rioch

70. Arsene Wenger

Records

71. 7-0 (vs. Middlesbrough, 2006)

72. 8-2 (vs. Manchester United, 2011)

73. Ted Drake (42 goals in 1934-35)

74. 49 games (across 2003-2004)

75. 10

76. 73,295 (vs. Sunderland, 1935)

77. 60,161 (vs. Manchester United, 2007)

78. 17

79. 7

80. 4 (shared by several players)

Current Squad

81. Martin Ødegaard

82. Kai Havertz

83. Bukayo Saka

84. Bukayo Saka

85. Gabriel Jesus

86. Martin Ødegaard

87. William Saliba

158. Nicklas Bendtner

159. Valencia

160. Unai Emery (2019 Europa League Final)

Premier League Era

161. 1992-93

162. 3

163. Ian Wright

164. Everton

165. Sylvain Wiltord

166. 2015-16

167. Newcastle United

168. Robin van Persie

169. Mikel Arteta

170. Arsene Wenger (2003-04)

Kits & Sponsors

171. Bruised Banana

172. Adidas

173. SEGA / Dreamcast

174. Blue and white lightning bolt design

175. 1980s (JVC)

176. Visit Rwanda

177. Yellow and navy

178. JVC

179. Emirates

88. Gabriel Martinelli 89. Leandro Trossard 90. Aaron Ramsdale Youth Academy 91. Hale End Academy 92. Per Mertesacker 93. Bukayo Saka 94. Ashley Cole 95. Emile Smith Rowe 96. Alex Iwobi 97. Mikel Arteta 98. 7 99. Bukayo Saka 100. Martin Keown	180. Pink and black Around the Club 181. Arsenal Foundation 182. Sir Chips Keswick 183. Arsenal Museum 184. London Colney, Hertfordshire 185. Arsenal Magazine 186. 1997 187. Arsenal Mastercard 188. Emirates 189. Arsenal Official App 190. Brian Eno Just for Fun 191. Jay Bothroyd 192. Thierry Henry 193. John Hartson 194. Arsene Wenger 195. David Rocastle 196. Emmanuel Eboué 197. Wojciech Szczęsny 198. Tony Adams 199. Andrey Arshavin (married to Yulia Arshavina) 200. Emmanuel Petit

Notebook Prompt: Use this space to jot down any new facts about football you learned from this section or ideas to share with other fans. You can also jot down any questions you have about these rules or how they apply in different game situations.

....

....

....

....

....

....

....

....

....

....

....

....

....

....

....

....

CHAPTER 8

Crossword Puzzle Games

Crossword 1

1. Arsenal's record goalscorer
2. Current Arsenal home ground
3. Arsenal's manager 1996-2018
4. Nickname for Arsenal
5. Former Arsenal midfielder, nicknamed "Rocky"
6. Arsenal's North London rivals
7. Invincibles' captain
8. Arsenal legend, wore the number 14 shirt
9. Former Arsenal goalkeeper, known for his eccentric style
10. Arsenal's home ground before Emirates Stadium
11. Arsenal's all-time top scorer in European competitions
12. Arsenal Ladies legend, with most appearances for the club
13. The year Arsenal was founded
14. Arsenal's manager 2018-2019
15. Former Arsenal midfielder, known for his passing ability
16. Arsenal striker who scored the winning goal in the 1989 title decider
17. Current Arsenal Women's manager

U	X	V	D	W	J	H	S	A	N	R	M	Y	S	J	F	Q	O	J	J
H	Z	S	R	E	N	N	U	G	N	B	C	G	E	G	H	N	B	I	G
I	H	Z	K	T	H	K	H	H	A	Q	W	F	R	I	E	O	I	U	I
S	G	X	R	E	I	Y	S	H	M	F	A	Y	I	H	G	N	G	V	E
I	I	S	K	O	X	R	M	J	H	H	V	O	P	B	D	A	R	K	T
L	I	W	E	N	G	E	R	T	E	S	A	H	F	I	P	I	O	A	K
L	V	S	J	U	M	I	G	Y	L	H	M	L	E	Y	Y	Z	S	V	R
F	N	Q	G	F	F	D	Q	Z	D	C	B	I	R	M	C	U	I	G	H
P	G	A	I	F	U	E	W	A	J	R	H	U	W	O	E	U	C	B	G
F	V	K	M	W	U	V	H	E	W	T	B	H	O	K	Z	R	K	X	C
E	J	O	D	P	S	A	N	F	O	H	X	L	Y	Q	P	A	Y	W	N
C	A	S	L	R	W	L	Y	C	G	R	B	X	A	S	R	E	C	I	A
J	B	X	W	U	F	L	X	I	C	W	E	M	I	R	A	T	E	S	L
U	J	X	P	Q	J	W	H	N	V	I	E	I	R	A	P	M	Y	L	D
L	W	F	T	W	R	T	W	E	V	V	V	U	U	I	H	G	O	F	T
F	X	D	K	K	T	G	Y	S	Q	C	B	E	F	P	W	H	C	H	L
Y	T	V	D	M	W	G	C	E	Z	V	J	Y	R	N	E	H	K	E	T
Y	N	U	Y	E	R	K	J	G	X	B	V	W	S	P	Y	X	E	N	K
H	6	8	8	1	P	E	I	E	B	Y	Y	N	U	S	A	I	D	R	W
X	F	B	O	J	O	U	S	Z	P	J	W	O	S	R	U	P	S	Y	X

Crossword 2

1. Arsenal's current manager
2. Former Arsenal striker, known for his pace
3. Arsenal's record signing
4. Arsenal's home ground 1913-2006
5. Former Arsenal left-back, known for his free kicks
6. Arsenal's current club captain
7. Invincibles' goalkeeper
8. Arsenal player who scored the winning goal in the 2014 and 2017 FA Cup Finals
9. Current Arsenal midfielder, nicknamed "Øde"
10. Arsenal's all-time appearance maker
11. Arsenal player who scored the winning goal in the 2020 FA Cup Final
12. Arsenal's manager 1986-1995
13. Arsenal's first Double-winning captain
14. Arsenal's current kit manufacturer
15. Former Arsenal midfielder, nicknamed "Super Jack"
16. Former Arsenal striker, known for his acrobatic celebrations
17. Arsenal's most successful manager in terms of trophies won

Y	R	A	E	L	'	O	E	Y	R	N	T	O	T	J	T	Y	W	J	D
H	J	E	K	B	V	F	O	F	A	H	D	B	Z	T	S	G	O	E	J
J	Z	A	C	I	B	Z	W	O	Z	S	I	R	J	J	O	R	L	M	V
Z	E	A	E	L	W	Z	C	Z	B	T	V	G	A	I	N	C	K	N	P
H	N	T	B	N	Q	R	T	S	T	K	Z	R	H	A	I	T	L	X	V
I	J	X	L	F	Y	U	U	S	O	W	X	U	C	B	G	K	H	A	M
W	Y	Z	E	O	Y	U	U	M	K	W	P	S	T	B	U	E	L	T	W
V	A	P	W	V	F	V	P	A	Y	B	J	F	O	D	A	R	D	X	H
R	R	O	G	L	G	J	L	D	S	E	T	I	G	D	N	T	Y	O	W
G	H	D	F	C	E	A	R	A	M	S	E	Y	G	U	R	M	S	H	S
U	N	P	L	V	P	T	E	I	X	U	E	A	M	V	U	Q	P	A	O
I	Z	N	Y	K	Z	E	D	E	F	I	U	O	W	M	B	G	I	W	K
B	F	R	A	I	E	T	M	A	X	B	M	D	W	Y	R	M	D	E	J
G	G	C	L	M	G	R	Y	Y	A	R	S	E	R	A	E	F	D	N	O
Q	T	M	B	Z	H	A	E	M	A	H	H	G	H	R	T	L	D	G	I
C	B	N	E	C	I	E	E	H	N	H	D	A	Y	A	N	D	K	E	O
X	E	H	C	U	O	Y	L	J	S	Z	M	A	X	T	I	L	A	R	X
C	A	D	I	D	A	S	E	X	S	L	S	R	E	M	W	W	F	A	T
N	B	L	R	N	J	A	Z	I	P	R	I	D	D	M	K	Q	M	Q	M
T	V	X	G	C	B	G	L	L	X	G	B	W	K	W	F	U	D	H	F

Crossword 3

1. Arsenal player who scored a hat-trick in the 2015 FA Cup Final
2. Former Arsenal midfielder, known for his powerful shots
3. Arsenal's current left-back
4. Arsenal's manager 1976-1983
5. Former Arsenal midfielder, known for his flair and creativity
6. The year Arsenal won their first league title
7. Arsenal's current shirt sponsor
8. Former Arsenal striker, known as "The Romford Pele"
9. Arsenal's goalkeeper in the 2004 Invincibles season
10. The month in which Arsenal traditionally play their home games at Emirates Stadium
11. Arsenal player who scored the winning goal in the 1971 Double-winning season
12. Former Arsenal defender, known for his tough tackling
13. Arsenal's first major trophy win
14. Arsenal's current kit manufacturer
15. Former Arsenal midfielder, nicknamed "Paddy"
16. Former Arsenal striker, known for his partnership with Ian Wright
17. Arsenal's manager 1925-1934

C	L	A	R	D	O	P	E	N	R	B	F	E	R	G	O	G	I	V	Z
S	Q	O	S	Q	O	U	I	U	S	R	K	M	T	W	R	B	D	P	Q
V	J	O	R	T	T	O	C	L	A	W	U	I	V	K	A	F	L	E	M
B	L	G	H	B	X	1	3	9	1	F	B	R	K	N	P	M	S	P	A
V	Z	R	G	R	E	B	G	N	U	J	L	A	A	L	L	I	Q	T	D
N	N	X	C	R	U	R	W	C	I	Q	X	T	Y	Z	B	S	Z	S	A
F	L	T	C	M	P	E	G	F	F	R	Z	E	W	U	A	R	L	N	M
S	D	J	I	N	H	S	G	K	R	H	A	S	M	L	Z	Z	E	V	S
L	T	E	R	K	I	V	J	Y	A	H	N	E	I	L	L	B	D	J	H
L	Z	E	X	D	Y	Q	N	E	N	M	Z	C	H	A	P	M	A	N	X
C	A	R	I	E	I	V	J	V	S	K	P	M	N	A	T	D	L	W	Q
F	E	Z	H	Z	I	N	C	H	E	N	K	O	A	C	S	R	W	P	D
F	H	R	J	Y	N	J	S	Z	R	F	B	N	C	F	O	H	Q	Q	B
K	Q	C	S	C	K	S	E	T	I	Z	S	J	H	U	O	P	T	L	A
J	Y	G	U	Q	X	K	E	G	P	A	I	E	A	U	A	I	I	V	S
Z	N	M	A	Y	D	C	J	V	D	N	A	S	R	R	S	H	N	A	F
X	D	E	D	R	F	M	J	I	S	R	W	K	L	E	G	Y	P	G	Q
B	T	K	Q	M	M	M	D	D	B	I	Y	O	T	V	S	G	X	Q	T
I	X	V	F	X	G	A	I	F	A	C	U	P	O	H	L	W	R	W	M
J	M	E	L	E	H	M	A	N	N	R	P	N	N	V	L	G	H	V	P

Crossword 4

1. Arsenal's all-time leading scorer in the Premier League
2. Former Arsenal right-back, known for his overlapping runs
3. Arsenal's current right-back
4. The year Arsenal moved to Emirates Stadium
5. Arsenal's manager 1966-1976
6. Former Arsenal striker, known for his clinical finishing
7. Arsenal's record appearance maker in European competitions
8. Arsenal player who scored the winning goal in the 2002 FA Cup Final
9. Arsenal's current number 10
10. The decade in which Arsenal won their first FA Cup
11. Arsenal player who scored a hat-trick against Tottenham Hotspur in 1993
12. Former Arsenal defender, known for his leadership qualities
13. Arsenal's nickname in the early 20th century
14. Arsenal's current sleeve sponsor
15. Former Arsenal midfielder, known for his long-range goals
16. Former Arsenal striker, known for his powerful heading ability
17. Arsenal's manager 1995-1996

G	X	2	0	0	6	E	K	J	L	U	I	D	Z	V	G	V	B	K	X
P	P	R	M	Y	G	G	L	W	O	I	N	P	T	F	Y	B	N	I	A
Y	R	D	R	S	L	O	L	X	E	T	I	H	W	V	A	J	D	M	W
G	Y	V	F	Y	E	Z	F	Z	S	B	E	T	I	S	D	R	J	R	U
J	J	P	C	E	X	Y	U	U	U	G	M	E	H	Q	A	S	T	I	W
L	M	J	I	Z	R	A	E	N	U	Y	I	P	W	N	M	K	H	O	V
H	P	H	F	K	D	S	K	N	O	R	V	H	G	A	S	A	G	C	J
V	V	M	V	Y	Z	S	N	P	A	R	I	A	B	F	A	Y	I	H	Y
Z	Q	I	S	Z	G	E	H	V	A	J	S	T	R	V	N	T	R	V	P
O	M	O	P	I	R	E	S	P	P	K	L	P	O	I	B	K	W	V	T
E	W	X	D	S	F	Z	M	P	O	H	K	A	N	S	K	L	G	G	G
L	P	H	Q	A	H	I	M	H	M	K	S	E	C	I	C	U	X	E	A
G	J	N	P	V	L	R	D	Q	M	C	T	W	L	T	T	M	P	Q	X
O	W	Y	N	B	P	G	V	V	E	E	C	Q	H	R	P	I	S	O	A
G	U	I	S	T	A	N	J	H	E	N	G	H	Q	W	C	C	A	H	A
W	D	D	K	H	F	F	Y	N	A	K	L	E	N	A	R	U	X	V	Y
W	F	L	Y	M	O	K	X	E	U	P	N	N	B	N	X	S	J	C	U
J	P	U	T	A	A	K	H	I	E	V	I	R	G	D	E	W	N	R	U
E	W	O	R	H	T	I	M	S	T	N	Y	Y	Y	A	H	I	I	X	J
K	J	B	P	X	F	S	U	E	H	V	W	Q	N	A	B	L	S	B	E

Crossword 5

1. Arsenal's current number 7
2. Former Arsenal goalkeeper, known for his penalty-saving abilities
3. Arsenal's current centre-back pairing
4. Arsenal's manager 2019-2021
5. Former Arsenal midfielder, known for his combative style
6. The year Arsenal won their first European trophy
7. Arsenal's home ground in the 19th century
8. Former Arsenal striker, known for his "flick and volley" goal against Newcastle United
9. Arsenal's current number 14
10. The number of FA Cups won by Arsenal
11. Arsenal player who scored the winning goal in the 1979 FA Cup Final
12. Former Arsenal defender, known for his long throws
13. Arsenal's first shirt sponsor
14. Arsenal's current goalkeeper
15. Former Arsenal midfielder, known for his dribbling skills
16. Former Arsenal striker, known for his partnership with Thierry Henry
17. Arsenal's manager 1934-1947

Q	S	O	Y	U	G	W	I	N	T	E	R	B	U	R	N	V	P	E	S
G	F	W	T	C	J	Z	H	H	S	V	W	B	P	L	Z	H	Z	K	R
Q	C	A	M	D	J	C	C	G	G	C	E	U	U	C	P	D	H	U	W
B	W	V	T	D	R	N	S	K	X	J	A	K	O	A	O	R	T	V	L
J	H	W	J	E	C	E	N	Q	X	V	H	U	V	E	D	O	O	Z	Y
E	A	O	C	H	A	E	T	H	I	R	C	I	Y	E	N	J	E	X	U
W	I	A	M	M	G	T	G	C	J	O	M	S	A	L	I	B	A	Z	R
J	T	E	A	V	M	R	J	M	B	V	H	U	R	W	K	Q	G	K	D
B	E	N	B	V	A	U	L	D	L	D	N	A	L	R	E	D	N	U	S
Q	K	H	C	H	N	O	E	A	N	X	I	F	Z	B	Q	L	B	W	M
Y	N	V	D	N	O	F	Q	I	Y	O	P	M	A	K	G	R	E	B	G
B	S	I	N	B	R	G	L	O	L	V	P	U	D	J	Y	X	U	K	R
B	Q	Q	C	K	G	G	Y	I	G	E	O	Q	C	A	F	R	B	L	A
4	K	K	J	A	R	N	Y	L	T	R	R	B	Z	Y	K	E	Z	D	M
9	Y	G	A	J	O	O	D	I	U	M	U	A	T	H	R	A	X	X	S
9	O	N	Z	V	U	S	T	N	C	A	B	W	Z	G	R	E	S	L	D
1	L	A	V	G	N	I	I	G	X	R	I	B	K	T	Q	T	E	H	A
N	J	Z	D	S	D	L	R	C	T	S	Y	A	E	M	G	I	I	I	L
I	S	J	D	I	Z	L	W	F	V	Y	M	T	A	K	O	Q	V	Y	E
V	A	Y	C	L	D	A	P	A	V	P	A	Q	B	W	F	C	V	I	R

Crossword 6

1. Arsenal player who scored the winning penalty in the 1993 FA Cup Final replay
2. Former Arsenal midfielder, known for his elegance and vision
3. Arsenal's current number 18
4. The year Arsenal won their first League Cup
5. Arsenal's manager 1958-1962
6. Former Arsenal striker, known for his powerful left foot
7. Arsenal's top scorer in the 1998 Double-winning season
8. Arsenal player who scored the winning goal in the 2015 FA Cup Final
9. Arsenal's current number 9
10. The decade in which Arsenal won their first European Cup Winners' Cup
11. Arsenal player who scored the winning goal in the 1987 League Cup Final
12. Former Arsenal defender, known for his versatility
13. Arsenal's nickname in the 1930s
14. Arsenal's current training ground
15. Former Arsenal midfielder, known for his goalscoring ability from midfield
16. Former Arsenal striker, known for his acrobatic goal celebrations
17. Arsenal's manager 1947-1953

R	F	H	G	K	S	F	F	P	L	Z	V	E	E	G	Y	A	W	F	W
V	L	P	N	E	U	J	H	N	B	H	T	J	Z	W	G	R	E	R	Z
R	D	Y	E	D	Q	R	V	A	Q	D	T	I	R	D	P	B	N	W	O
G	M	K	A	E	K	U	M	L	F	L	O	Z	X	L	K	T	J	E	V
C	B	U	H	V	K	Y	B	O	Y	S	C	A	Y	O	W	Q	W	L	H
K	B	A	O	U	T	P	W	N	M	N	L	U	X	C	D	Q	A	B	C
P	M	A	K	G	R	E	B	D	G	I	A	H	D	B	S	S	E	E	F
D	L	H	N	F	P	J	C	O	V	D	W	I	M	E	N	Q	X	C	X
U	V	S	C	K	J	U	P	N	T	N	L	U	G	Y	K	S	M	K	K
J	E	S	U	S	O	U	J	C	Y	I	C	G	Z	N	B	C	L	R	I
B	T	B	S	C	N	F	T	O	O	W	U	B	I	X	U	S	H	A	W
S	K	J	E	C	W	X	E	L	E	S	U	H	K	R	N	F	P	J	H
P	S	H	Y	F	B	X	H	N	T	J	N	H	P	V	N	A	F	N	O
K	N	X	T	I	U	I	F	E	G	D	Q	U	G	Z	K	S	W	E	M
V	E	J	S	H	W	G	R	Y	I	L	V	A	R	L	N	N	W	E	E
K	E	R	H	S	L	P	Q	C	S	J	A	B	E	W	J	I	N	T	R
E	D	A	R	P	U	G	K	D	H	I	K	N	O	M	T	V	Q	E	S
P	N	G	E	I	L	S	I	E	A	U	A	E	D	O	D	C	V	N	O
T	W	G	T	Y	C	M	E	Q	G	G	K	F	B	S	I	O	A	I	N
R	F	7	8	9	1	R	I	J	F	K	R	A	T	P	T	T	P	N	H

Crossword 7

1. Arsenal's current number 11
2. Former Arsenal goalkeeper, known for his consistency and reliability
3. Arsenal's current central midfield pairing
4. The year Arsenal completed an unbeaten Premier League season
5. Arsenal's manager 1962-1966
6. Former Arsenal striker, known for his clinical finishing and composure
7. Arsenal's captain in the 2004 Invincibles season
8. Arsenal player who scored the winning goal in the 2003 FA Cup Final
9. Arsenal's current number 8
10. The number of Premier League titles won by Arsenal
11. Arsenal player who scored the winning goal in the 1991 title-winning season
12. Former Arsenal defender, known for his aerial ability
13. Arsenal's first ever manager
14. Arsenal's current women's captain
15. Former Arsenal midfielder, known for his passing range and vision
16. Former Arsenal striker, known for his partnership with Dennis Bergkamp
17. Arsenal's manager 1953-1958

O	Y	D	K	R	P	O	C	Y	R	N	E	H	S	Z	C	U	V	P	Q
Y	Z	Q	H	E	J	C	A	E	J	G	X	U	I	P	D	G	P	C	C
Q	F	U	V	U	B	N	A	K	H	O	K	I	C	F	D	G	J	O	Q
K	Q	X	O	X	Z	I	Q	M	T	I	W	K	W	P	P	L	W	I	G
F	E	A	I	S	K	P	P	H	P	K	V	F	S	C	I	I	J	L	I
U	M	G	R	L	Q	B	D	J	L	B	U	T	N	W	M	R	V	O	A
C	E	O	C	U	E	V	L	W	Z	W	E	S	Q	I	S	Q	E	S	D
B	E	F	F	K	S	M	F	S	Y	P	N	L	A	L	T	R	M	S	R
A	W	H	I	T	T	A	K	E	R	M	W	K	L	L	M	T	M	U	J
J	R	F	F	B	M	H	E	F	A	O	G	L	E	I	N	O	V	J	O
A	I	O	Z	T	M	G	U	R	V	I	E	I	R	A	U	H	B	V	F
T	G	D	Y	E	A	N	T	J	J	F	W	F	O	M	E	N	D	Q	G
J	H	L	Q	D	X	I	M	X	Q	P	S	T	T	S	H	I	L	P	M
D	T	W	Y	C	N	K	W	G	A	M	A	H	B	O	I	G	A	Y	V
V	J	W	M	E	U	C	E	J	V	D	G	X	T	N	B	R	M	Y	O
R	Q	I	L	X	I	U	J	N	D	I	E	H	Y	F	T	O	U	D	U
B	X	L	Y	N	Q	B	X	J	R	R	R	W	T	E	D	J	V	P	C
N	I	S	A	4	0	0	2	W	G	E	B	Z	Y	I	H	U	D	Q	F
L	D	O	G	C	M	A	P	R	E	J	A	T	Q	L	M	H	V	P	F
E	A	N	R	N	U	Y	N	F	R	N	F	P	D	B	L	S	O	J	V

Crossword 8

1. Arsenal's current number 10
2. Former Arsenal goalkeeper, known for his shot-stopping ability
3. Arsenal's current attacking trio
4. The year Arsenal won their first FA Cup double
5. Arsenal's manager 1983-1986
6. Former Arsenal striker, known for his pace and dribbling skills
7. Arsenal's captain in the 1991 title-winning season
8. Arsenal player who scored the winning goal in the 2005 FA Cup Final
9. Arsenal's current number 4
10. The number of trophies won by Arsène Wenger as Arsenal manager
11. Arsenal player who scored the winning goal in the 1998 FA Cup Final
12. Former Arsenal defender, known for his tough tackling and no-nonsense approach
13. Arsenal's home ground before moving to Highbury
14. Arsenal's stadium announcer
15. Former Arsenal midfielder, known for his creativity and passing ability
16. Former Arsenal striker, known for his "one-nil to the Arsenal" chant
17. Arsenal's manager 1939-1945

U	V	W	R	E	C	R	X	W	N	Q	U	Z	G	H	H	L	M	F	W
M	B	H	H	K	W	L	O	V	E	R	M	A	R	S	I	Y	Q	E	N
M	A	R	T	I	N	E	L	L	I	Q	H	S	L	R	V	X	Z	Q	E
S	N	K	Z	Y	T	G	M	O	P	P	J	X	G	A	D	N	J	I	U
M	L	H	G	X	F	T	W	F	J	U	O	K	F	M	Q	K	L	I	A
R	O	R	J	G	M	H	A	D	A	M	S	Z	A	R	P	E	E	E	S
N	W	D	X	B	I	C	P	K	Z	M	M	X	L	E	H	M	A	N	N
R	U	E	E	T	R	U	X	K	E	O	A	L	Q	V	Z	O	D	V	F
Y	S	V	E	G	P	V	D	H	P	R	J	C	L	O	J	O	M	F	M
L	R	S	P	I	A	S	E	C	K	G	Q	L	K	P	E	T	C	M	J
L	D	T	B	H	U	A	V	C	A	Z	O	R	L	A	R	H	N	U	W
B	Z	N	A	Y	C	F	R	O	R	K	S	F	M	G	E	E	P	M	H
P	L	U	M	S	T	E	A	D	C	O	M	M	O	N	M	G	M	V	O
L	F	L	C	I	X	Z	H	A	I	H	V	Z	H	O	Y	G	D	G	V
S	K	S	M	A	D	A	V	D	R	V	H	T	H	I	R	T	E	E	N
O	E	W	O	H	E	I	X	A	A	I	B	B	N	Y	O	P	M	X	Z
P	Y	V	K	B	L	T	Y	M	U	E	F	E	3	B	Y	F	F	K	P
C	D	O	Z	R	T	T	R	S	D	I	H	V	9	W	L	O	V	T	C
Q	L	U	N	C	I	E	T	R	Q	R	G	U	9	E	E	U	E	U	Y
U	U	J	N	D	Q	V	Q	G	P	A	J	F	1	Y	E	B	V	E	J

Crossword 9

1. Arsenal's current number 1
2. Former Arsenal midfielder, known for his "Invincibles" goal against Liverpool
3. Arsenal's current left-back
4. The year Arsenal won the FA Cup and League Cup double
5. Arsenal's manager 1919-1925
6. Former Arsenal striker, known for his goalscoring record in the 1930s
7. Arsenal's top scorer in all competitions
8. Arsenal player who scored the winning goal in the 2017 FA Cup Final
9. Arsenal's current number 20
10. The decade in which Arsenal won their first league and FA Cup double
11. Arsenal player who scored the winning goal in the 1993 FA Cup Final replay
12. Former Arsenal defender, known for his partnership with Tony Adams
13. Arsenal's mascot
14. Arsenal's official charity
15. Former Arsenal midfielder, known for his technical ability and passing range
16. Former Arsenal striker, known for his "twisted blood" celebration
17. Arsenal's manager 1915-1919

C	Y	Q	A	N	J	P	W	P	1	S	P	A	R	S	L	Z	P	J	Y
E	V	I	O	C	E	R	P	9	Q	U	D	X	K	Y	M	N	F	G	J
A	V	B	T	N	G	E	9	Y	A	F	E	Z	J	N	C	S	H	O	Q
X	R	O	A	C	A	3	T	G	R	K	Z	G	G	L	J	Z	U	K	G
T	K	S	A	I	H	H	Y	E	V	N	N	T	N	T	E	P	R	N	U
T	X	Y	E	S	M	A	R	Y	N	E	E	S	N	P	T	Z	V	E	N
W	T	N	S	N	F	L	D	T	A	I	Q	H	M	R	I	E	N	H	N
J	V	B	C	A	A	P	H	I	C	V	N	A	G	F	J	P	H	C	E
O	G	B	D	B	D	L	U	O	B	Z	K	O	H	O	Q	L	E	N	R
H	E	N	R	Y	Q	D	F	T	G	G	R	E	R	O	U	G	U	I	S
Q	N	O	R	V	W	O	G	O	R	A	R	G	Z	Y	S	A	Q	Z	A
L	C	T	U	H	R	O	N	E	U	G	I	V	J	S	N	K	K	I	U
P	L	H	C	C	H	Y	B	Y	D	N	W	E	N	K	U	S	V	N	R
S	W	G	N	F	R	H	N	N	H	E	D	L	E	C	I	P	F	U	U
P	T	I	F	B	P	T	R	O	K	Q	D	A	K	I	C	M	M	A	S
H	E	N	R	Y	W	B	S	A	V	U	S	D	T	D	F	W	F	M	R
M	W	K	X	C	E	N	R	L	A	J	C	S	T	I	Q	I	G	D	E
N	Z	H	B	T	F	D	X	A	N	R	H	M	K	S	O	R	S	K	X
V	C	A	K	T	N	R	O	P	V	J	E	A	Z	O	I	N	J	G	J
N	B	E	L	H	D	A	M	U	Y	P	Z	R	F	M	O	L	A	M	S

Crossword 10

1. Arsenal's current number 23
2. Former Arsenal goalkeeper, known for his long kicks
3. Arsenal's current centre-back pairing
4. The year Arsenal won their second European trophy
5. Arsenal's manager 1976-1983
6. Former Arsenal striker, known for his pace and clinical finishing
7. Arsenal's captain in the 2002 Double-winning season
8. Arsenal player who scored the winning goal in the 2020 FA Cup Final
9. Arsenal's current number 21
10. The number of FA Cup final appearances by Arsenal
11. Arsenal player who scored the winning goal in the 2014 FA Cup Final
12. Former Arsenal defender, known for his leadership and defensive solidity
13. Arsenal's first major trophy win after World War II
14. Arsenal's current sleeve sponsor
15. Former Arsenal midfielder, known for his powerful shots and long-range goals
16. Former Arsenal striker, known for his partnership with Nicolas Anelka
17. Arsenal's manager 1925-1934

F	H	F	X	X	U	M	A	Q	A	B	I	B	O	Q	Q	W	P	C	S
I	H	E	N	R	Y	P	W	L	A	A	T	O	M	I	Y	A	S	U	W
U	X	W	X	A	U	R	D	Y	N	O	N	I	Z	E	J	O	O	M	R
A	D	N	A	W	R	T	I	S	I	V	L	Z	S	N	P	T	H	F	B
X	R	R	S	C	V	I	E	I	R	A	S	M	Z	K	O	L	U	V	V
N	S	U	G	H	K	S	Z	F	R	M	A	K	S	K	E	Z	G	M	S
O	V	H	C	A	D	I	G	Y	E	R	H	O	S	I	G	D	G	U	U
U	W	E	X	P	H	M	V	U	J	V	R	E	R	V	A	R	E	I	V
X	W	V	K	M	G	Y	V	A	D	V	Z	B	E	R	G	K	A	M	P
L	E	H	M	A	N	N	Q	Y	O	F	A	E	K	E	K	V	W	K	N
Q	K	R	J	N	A	M	V	G	A	G	B	L	J	C	G	X	S	S	A
G	L	C	P	I	Y	V	B	Y	Z	R	C	Z	L	T	W	E	N	T	Y
R	S	X	X	G	E	B	O	G	I	N	F	Y	K	I	C	O	V	P	O
E	M	U	S	T	M	D	B	I	U	I	J	T	Z	S	E	I	D	L	J
B	A	P	A	J	A	I	P	R	S	T	W	P	Q	M	I	N	E	K	O
G	D	H	U	H	B	G	K	V	M	I	4	B	K	Q	N	X	J	E	I
N	A	F	R	C	U	P	W	T	X	E	9	S	F	U	B	L	Q	A	P
U	Q	P	A	C	A	O	A	I	F	G	9	Q	N	H	G	T	Q	H	G
J	P	K	T	N	X	F	K	P	H	J	1	Q	I	W	G	U	I	P	K
L	Z	C	E	W	X	D	V	O	M	V	B	O	L	W	F	X	F	K	O

Crossword 11

1. Arsenal player who scored a hat-trick in the 2003 FA Cup Final
2. Former Arsenal midfielder, known for his combative style and tackling ability
3. Arsenal's current right-back
4. The year Arsenal moved to Emirates Stadium
5. Arsenal's manager 1966-1976
6. Former Arsenal striker, known for his clinical finishing and predatory instincts
7. Arsenal's record appearance maker in the Premier League
8. Arsenal player who scored the winning goal in the 1979 FA Cup Final
9. Arsenal's current number 7
10. The decade in which Arsenal won their first League Cup
11. Arsenal player who scored a hat-trick against Tottenham Hotspur in 1996
12. Former Arsenal defender, known for his pace and strength
13. Arsenal's nickname in the early 20th century
14. Arsenal's current women's manager
15. Former Arsenal midfielder, known for his long-range goals and free kicks
16. Former Arsenal striker, known for his powerful heading ability
17. Arsenal's manager 1995-1996

B	A	K	I	F	K	C	I	L	Y	O	R	X	C	G	Y	T	L	Y	G
P	Y	B	F	C	A	S	A	K	A	S	U	N	D	E	R	L	A	N	D
N	R	R	L	H	A	I	Q	X	T	N	P	U	O	T	G	L	W	K	D
L	E	U	L	H	S	A	V	S	V	X	R	O	O	W	V	A	M	A	O
2	T	E	F	G	C	X	M	M	K	Z	I	R	V	K	F	V	F	Z	D
Y	0	Z	T	U	P	A	I	X	O	R	O	Z	A	J	S	E	Q	D	T
F	K	0	E	E	D	P	M	O	Q	X	C	Y	W	M	T	D	V	N	P
I	P	C	6	A	N	V	K	P	K	A	H	J	H	P	W	I	K	I	Y
N	G	X	T	D	J	I	X	V	B	N	U	S	I	X	M	E	R	P	L
P	V	B	F	I	I	S	N	Z	H	E	W	X	T	B	K	E	N	F	A
N	E	Q	L	I	O	R	J	P	W	L	L	L	E	G	S	W	N	A	G
R	Y	O	C	T	A	E	A	N	Z	K	A	L	W	K	S	Q	D	A	W
X	M	W	A	P	I	N	D	T	Z	A	W	R	R	I	Z	G	K	R	Y
S	E	B	M	U	A	N	D	G	I	Z	B	Q	I	M	X	C	R	X	D
C	E	I	U	D	L	U	O	B	W	P	X	B	X	E	W	A	R	P	X
H	L	B	W	R	I	G	H	T	D	C	A	N	D	L	I	Q	K	X	L
B	I	S	I	Q	N	E	J	L	B	L	L	Q	S	C	L	V	G	K	G
E	E	V	Q	H	V	H	X	P	V	Y	V	U	V	W	F	Q	B	I	S
W	B	M	W	R	P	T	T	K	L	B	T	G	O	O	Z	D	M	F	R
F	P	P	N	F	L	X	F	B	U	Y	U	Z	A	Y	H	L	Q	A	F

Crossword 12

1. Arsenal's current number 14
2. Former Arsenal goalkeeper, known for his eccentric personality and saves
3. Arsenal's current central midfield pairing
4. The year Arsenal won their first Premier League title
5. Arsenal's manager 1986-1995
6. Former Arsenal striker, known for his clinical finishing and composure
7. Arsenal's captain in the 1998 Double-winning season
8. Arsenal player who scored the winning goal in the 2017 FA Cup Final
9. Arsenal's current number 2
10. The number of trophies won by Arsène Wenger as Arsenal manager
11. Arsenal player who scored the winning goal in the 2002 FA Cup Final
12. Former Arsenal defender, known for his leadership and defensive solidity
13. Arsenal's first major trophy win after World War II
14. Arsenal's current sleeve sponsor
15. Former Arsenal midfielder, known for his powerful shots and long-range goals
16. Former Arsenal striker, known for his partnership with Nicolas Anelka
17. Arsenal's manager 1925-1934

G	R	H	E	K	F	B	R	F	S	H	R	O	I	W	I	K	I	B	O
K	S	J	V	D	S	S	T	K	C	D	X	D	M	M	Q	T	M	S	S
N	R	G	K	G	O	I	Q	Z	R	T	T	O	T	G	O	J	Q	W	Q
M	Q	P	D	C	B	M	H	N	A	M	P	A	H	C	E	Z	D	K	A
V	S	R	I	E	J	P	R	V	N	W	D	K	A	U	B	F	D	L	Y
I	A	S	P	D	U	M	E	L	P	M	N	J	E	D	H	E	Q	K	E
S	K	F	J	A	F	A	L	O	J	U	D	C	O	X	A	K	K	J	N
I	P	P	P	T	V	K	C	B	T	U	C	W	B	S	F	M	O	P	R
T	T	H	H	I	X	G	Q	U	A	N	N	A	M	H	E	L	S	W	K
R	R	I	Z	Z	R	R	V	M	B	P	A	G	F	O	G	Q	A	T	U
W	T	M	N	N	K	E	T	I	A	H	Y	A	B	T	E	X	H	Q	S
A	S	U	C	D	R	B	S	Q	D	C	U	G	E	E	S	I	A	Y	O
N	X	Z	A	U	G	H	E	H	1	9	9	8	R	N	R	S	X	G	D
D	A	W	M	P	S	M	D	Q	G	H	X	R	D	T	F	G	M	Q	F
A	J	P	Y	A	B	G	V	A	E	C	Y	J	E	A	N	V	H	D	G
W	G	H	R	R	H	V	A	N	J	Q	K	E	E	D	C	R	U	I	G
S	O	R	H	T	L	A	R	U	X	M	N	N	S	A	B	D	H	F	F
Q	Z	I	R	E	Z	Y	R	X	H	O	Z	M	M	M	T	P	D	Q	A
Y	B	J	M	Y	C	Q	F	G	M	R	T	O	D	S	A	E	K	E	S
C	P	F	B	M	N	E	T	S	B	Y	G	L	U	P	H	R	W	R	S

Crossword 13

1. Arsenal player who scored a hat-trick in the 1991 title-winning season
2. Former Arsenal midfielder, known for his flair and creativity
3. Arsenal's current left-back
4. The year Arsenal won the FA Cup and League Cup double
5. Arsenal's manager 1919-1925
6. Former Arsenal striker, known for his goalscoring record in the 1930s
7. Arsenal's top scorer in all competitions
8. Arsenal player who scored the winning goal in the 2015 FA Cup Final
9. Arsenal's current number 20
10. The decade in which Arsenal won their first league and FA Cup double
11. Arsenal player who scored the winning goal in the 1993 FA Cup Final
12. Former Arsenal defender, known for his partnership with Tony Adams
13. Arsenal's mascot
14. Arsenal's official charity
15. Former Arsenal midfielder, known for his technical ability and passing range
16. Former Arsenal striker, known for his "twisted blood" celebration
17. Arsenal's manager 1915-1919

C	N	D	A	L	N	Q	N	X	X	I	L	H	M	U	W	M	Q	Q	V
U	L	I	R	F	S	K	C	I	D	L	L	J	C	N	X	T	N	H	M
X	J	N	S	B	A	K	P	W	B	A	Q	H	T	M	N	T	P	P	P
Y	D	E	E	H	P	Q	U	F	W	Z	E	W	T	S	I	W	N	I	C
X	X	E	N	F	C	D	B	Y	R	N	E	H	T	Q	Q	W	O	G	R
V	N	T	A	F	Z	H	E	N	R	Y	C	U	O	T	X	N	N	O	N
N	C	E	L	H	N	Y	L	Y	J	P	I	V	C	S	O	I	D	T	X
F	H	N	F	L	W	V	H	S	H	G	W	A	L	E	E	A	A	N	M
Y	S	I	O	K	K	W	T	F	R	V	Q	U	A	Y	F	W	J	V	O
P	B	N	U	K	A	Q	S	A	S	N	R	E	W	X	N	S	A	F	K
G	U	N	N	E	R	S	A	U	R	U	S	R	E	X	G	R	P	R	N
X	A	X	D	E	A	L	I	A	F	D	H	C	X	D	L	X	S	X	E
P	D	H	A	V	K	B	Z	H	S	O	P	V	U	K	P	C	P	F	H
V	V	3	T	P	J	A	C	H	E	B	S	Q	N	P	J	I	C	D	C
M	L	9	I	I	T	C	R	R	U	H	I	I	D	M	Y	Y	A	H	N
V	U	9	O	R	M	O	Y	D	N	U	G	V	A	P	R	Z	J	P	I
G	X	1	N	E	J	S	P	L	D	H	F	N	A	Z	R	H	O	M	Z
S	U	X	M	S	L	Y	K	U	T	S	C	O	O	M	O	B	Y	V	N
X	J	U	J	N	D	K	L	O	J	O	R	G	I	N	H	O	M	C	F
L	C	A	Y	Q	L	V	N	B	V	K	E	E	M	P	A	P	D	C	Q

Crossword 14

1. Arsenal's current number 1
2. Former Arsenal midfielder, known for his "Invincibles" goal against Liverpool
3. Arsenal's current centre-back pairing
4. The year Arsenal won their second European trophy
5. Arsenal's manager 1976-1983
6. Former Arsenal striker, known for his pace and clinical finishing
7. Arsenal's captain in the 2002 Double-winning season
8. Arsenal player who scored the winning goal in the 2020 FA Cup Final
9. Arsenal's current number 21
10. The number of FA Cup final appearances by Arsenal
11. Arsenal player who scored the winning goal in the 2014 FA Cup Final
12. Former Arsenal defender, known for his leadership and defensive solidity
13. Arsenal's first major trophy win after World War II
14. Arsenal's current kit manufacturer
15. Former Arsenal midfielder, known for his powerful shots and long-range goals
16. Former Arsenal striker, known for his partnership with Nicolas Anelka
17. Arsenal's manager 1925-1934

O	J	X	A	H	M	I	C	U	Q	Y	T	N	E	W	T	O	M	E	U
G	Y	E	S	M	A	R	B	P	Z	F	J	A	N	I	O	J	H	U	V
R	Z	P	M	O	D	Y	F	P	V	N	Z	U	Z	Q	P	K	E	S	T
K	V	P	Y	Y	V	N	P	F	M	K	C	D	D	A	E	T	N	P	U
E	C	W	K	I	Z	A	J	P	M	A	K	G	R	E	B	C	R	X	R
L	H	G	Z	H	J	O	D	S	J	L	K	I	M	T	R	G	Y	G	L
A	X	I	B	D	H	T	A	A	M	A	S	G	N	F	Q	T	A	X	G
D	L	E	P	O	N	L	S	G	M	K	K	A	R	E	U	V	U	U	L
S	K	E	E	A	I	M	U	A	W	S	W	G	D	E	K	C	E	O	X
M	U	B	U	B	O	T	Y	G	J	Z	O	Z	M	I	B	O	L	C	F
A	U	B	A	M	E	Y	A	N	G	T	S	D	X	Y	D	K	L	X	S
R	L	J	U	N	G	B	E	R	G	I	L	O	X	S	X	A	J	Z	U
Q	1	9	9	4	F	E	Y	P	R	Q	Y	Z	Z	D	B	K	S	V	O
O	W	B	N	C	A	G	L	O	S	B	G	N	E	I	L	L	I	I	S
Z	C	H	A	P	M	A	N	H	Y	Z	P	G	G	H	P	L	Q	Q	B
Y	S	C	G	G	R	Q	N	G	B	T	X	W	B	W	Q	X	H	P	D
J	J	M	G	I	A	M	Z	A	L	J	Z	Z	P	I	O	U	U	Z	F
W	P	U	E	S	A	V	R	P	X	V	V	W	R	L	W	C	Y	K	E
G	O	I	I	J	V	V	I	E	R	A	W	M	Z	M	A	G	W	B	T
D	V	P	Q	Q	J	O	E	L	P	A	S	S	A	F	J	R	G	D	Q

Crossword 15

1. Arsenal player who scored a hat-trick in the 2003 FA Cup Final
2. Former Arsenal midfielder, known for his combative style and tackling ability
3. Arsenal's current right-back
4. The year Arsenal moved to Emirates Stadium
5. Arsenal's manager 1966-1976
6. Former Arsenal striker, known for his clinical finishing and predatory instincts
7. Arsenal's record appearance maker in the Premier League
8. Arsenal player who scored the winning goal in the 1979 FA Cup Final
9. Arsenal's current number 7
10. The decade in which Arsenal won their first League Cup
11. Arsenal player who scored a hat-trick against Tottenham Hotspur in 1996
12. Former Arsenal defender, known for his pace and strength
13. Arsenal's nickname in the early 20th century
14. Arsenal's current women's manager
15. Former Arsenal midfielder, known for his long-range goals and free kicks
16. 1 Former Arsenal striker, known for his powerful heading ability
17. Arsenal's manager 1995-1996

U	Y	D	G	D	Z	K	Z	C	H	N	L	P	F	C	K	D	T	P	Q
D	E	S	D	I	R	Z	X	A	U	K	S	U	D	H	I	I	A	R	M
J	G	A	R	H	Y	C	X	S	D	P	E	M	K	T	S	S	A	V	Q
L	X	K	N	A	B	R	L	M	K	B	R	U	K	L	W	P	A	P	E
L	E	A	I	U	S	L	J	O	D	X	K	L	I	O	M	C	E	O	T
C	U	I	J	V	A	M	W	N	F	S	W	U	Y	I	B	R	S	K	H
D	B	E	X	V	F	C	A	M	P	B	E	L	L	X	J	R	G	I	D
A	L	I	E	U	D	L	B	D	A	F	U	N	Z	N	A	U	W	I	L
U	N	D	J	E	R	T	C	J	A	B	J	O	V	X	M	G	I	X	U
U	I	E	Z	E	B	T	Y	T	K	S	K	G	V	X	T	V	H	U	O
E	V	F	D	S	D	X	H	U	H	O	E	P	T	I	N	G	C	U	B
O	X	N	R	A	H	C	6	E	Q	G	W	R	W	F	E	K	O	D	E
Y	U	B	M	E	E	H	D	0	G	C	I	M	I	K	E	I	I	A	S
S	L	Y	C	T	P	U	E	W	0	U	E	R	A	P	T	O	R	Z	L
D	D	I	R	I	X	O	U	Y	R	2	N	N	W	F	E	J	Q	A	Z
Z	E	U	A	H	T	U	T	Z	E	Z	E	N	Q	F	N	U	V	B	Q
X	S	S	O	W	P	V	W	U	A	L	K	U	E	N	I	A	E	S	Z
Y	R	S	C	B	W	U	M	B	K	P	J	J	B	R	N	Y	S	A	Y
O	V	A	K	H	U	Y	F	A	A	B	Z	L	C	U	S	Z	K	S	G
B	Q	H	Y	D	J	N	P	N	U	J	K	K	O	T	G	N	N	B	H

Crossword 16

1. Current Arsenal midfielder, wears the number 19 shirt
2. Former Arsenal striker, scored the winning goal in the 1993 FA Cup Final
3. Arsenal's current first-choice goalkeeper
4. The year Arsenal won their first European trophy
5. Former Arsenal manager, known for his "boring, boring Arsenal" quote
6. Former Arsenal striker, known for his partnership with Ian Wright
7. Arsenal's record appearance maker in European competitions
8. Arsenal player who scored the winning goal in the 2005 FA Cup Final
9. Current Arsenal defender, wears the number 6 shirt
10. Number of goals scored by Arsenal in the 2003-04 "Invincibles" season
11. Arsenal player who scored the winning goal in the 1998 FA Cup Final
12. Former Arsenal defender, known for his tough tackling and disciplinary record
13. Arsenal's home ground before moving to Highbury
14. Current Arsenal Women's manager
15. Former Arsenal midfielder, known for his creativity and passing ability
16. Former Arsenal striker, known for his "one-nil to the Arsenal" chant
17. Arsenal's manager between 1939-1945

S	R	F	I	Y	O	S	J	A	D	A	M	S	N	O	J	F	J	V	R
E	E	M	A	G	P	K	E	O	V	E	R	M	A	R	S	Y	G	R	F
M	K	J	Y	U	L	C	O	G	I	E	G	W	C	R	J	Y	U	J	E
J	A	O	Z	H	U	I	K	B	Y	R	Y	B	J	S	J	O	O	E	F
H	T	C	P	Y	M	D	S	X	B	H	Z	H	G	U	E	A	J	A	R
T	T	A	R	K	S	G	A	X	P	T	B	R	C	G	D	F	R	V	G
P	I	Y	S	I	T	F	B	Q	H	Y	A	E	Z	L	E	M	I	I	L
U	H	J	M	F	E	T	G	D	X	T	L	W	R	O	M	M	E	E	E
B	W	P	A	E	A	G	R	X	Z	N	E	F	U	S	Z	M	I	I	B
C	P	L	D	U	D	R	V	L	E	E	L	V	R	X	P	R	D	R	X
K	Y	F	A	H	C	A	A	N	R	V	A	W	B	N	B	K	E	A	B
U	M	E	L	T	O	H	Y	B	Z	E	D	M	P	A	L	V	V	F	L
N	B	L	X	O	M	A	C	E	I	S	S	P	G	C	U	T	A	H	O
D	Y	V	I	B	M	M	F	B	T	B	M	E	R	F	K	C	L	Q	F
V	B	Y	O	O	O	P	V	L	K	A	A	U	H	E	T	A	L	W	Y
N	K	E	O	W	N	U	Z	K	K	A	R	I	H	C	C	Z	S	U	P
I	E	V	1	9	9	4	G	G	N	X	N	L	O	Q	A	O	Y	F	Z
E	H	H	N	D	S	Q	R	T	I	U	J	O	A	N	M	R	T	W	S
V	T	U	G	M	W	E	P	V	C	U	Z	O	C	F	R	L	Z	Q	W
W	V	U	W	A	B	R	V	F	H	K	V	U	Y	U	F	A	G	K	L

Crossword 17

1. Current Arsenal midfielder, wears the number 8 shirt
2. Former Arsenal goalkeeper, known for his penalty-saving abilities in the 2003 FA Cup Final
3. Arsenal's current attacking trio
4. The year Arsenal won their first FA Cup double
5. Former Arsenal manager, managed the club between 1983-1986
6. Former Arsenal striker, known for his pace and dribbling skills
7. Arsenal's captain in the 1991 title-winning season
8. Arsenal player who scored the winning goal in the 2005 FA Cup Final
9. Current Arsenal defender, wears the number 4 shirt
10. Number of Premier League titles won by Arsenal
11. Arsenal player who scored the winning goal in the 1998 FA Cup Final
12. Former Arsenal defender, known for his tough tackling and no-nonsense approach
13. Arsenal's home ground before moving to Highbury
14. Arsenal's current stadium announcer
15. Former Arsenal midfielder, known for his creativity and passing ability
16. Former Arsenal striker, known for his "one-nil to the Arsenal" chant
17. Arsenal's all-time top scorer

L	I	F	J	U	K	T	U	R	K	S	G	T	A	F	X	B	C	B	X
J	A	S	U	S	E	J	D	Z	B	Q	F	E	N	Z	K	Z	Z	J	O
H	E	H	I	G	O	Z	Y	Q	A	D	A	M	S	M	A	D	A	T	L
H	M	G	H	R	T	Z	R	K	P	V	I	H	M	P	Z	O	X	U	C
P	K	C	V	O	O	V	N	C	H	V	X	H	A	X	J	V	Q	C	R
H	T	S	E	S	W	M	E	E	A	Q	J	G	D	Y	O	E	J	E	P
T	C	J	J	Y	X	E	H	E	E	Z	G	K	A	P	S	R	W	R	X
K	V	C	C	K	V	R	T	J	L	R	O	B	Z	T	Q	M	C	G	S
F	J	S	L	U	H	H	E	I	N	N	H	R	H	J	O	A	C	E	J
B	F	3	A	V	O	Q	F	A	H	A	V	T	L	O	T	R	E	E	O
R	N	H	9	L	H	H	M	M	W	W	M	I	Y	A	N	S	C	M	V
B	Z	I	B	9	B	K	N	Y	R	W	Q	A	O	Q	S	L	T	F	E
X	Q	W	S	N	1	W	Z	I	V	N	Y	A	E	R	V	C	Y	Z	R
H	I	D	O	Q	A	E	K	M	G	A	P	T	D	S	Q	B	W	Y	M
L	W	E	L	Y	O	R	Y	M	E	R	E	J	T	Y	G	S	Y	V	A
U	C	A	N	C	I	B	I	Z	O	A	O	N	O	O	M	E	O	H	R
I	Q	O	H	D	P	D	K	E	B	B	W	J	K	V	V	X	Q	Z	S
R	G	Q	Y	A	X	W	R	E	I	O	X	E	D	Z	Y	V	M	Q	P
W	P	T	B	O	D	R	C	A	L	V	V	J	S	M	K	Q	J	Y	R
P	L	U	M	S	T	E	A	D	C	O	M	M	O	N	R	I	J	I	Z

Crossword 18

1. Current Arsenal midfielder, wears the number 10 shirt
2. Former Arsenal goalkeeper, known for his consistency and reliability
3. Arsenal's current central midfield pairing
4. The year Arsenal completed an unbeaten Premier League season
5. Former Arsenal manager, managed the club between 1962-1966
6. Former Arsenal striker, known for his clinical finishing and composure
7. Arsenal's captain in the 2004 Invincibles season
8. Arsenal player who scored the winning goal in the 2003 FA Cup Final
9. Current Arsenal defender, wears the number 12 shirt
10. The number of FA Cups won by Arsenal
11. Arsenal player who scored the winning goal in the 1991 title-winning season
12. Former Arsenal defender, known for his aerial ability and goalscoring prowess
13. Arsenal's first ever manager
14. Arsenal's current women's captain
15. Former Arsenal midfielder, known for his passing range and vision
16. Former Arsenal striker, known for his partnership with Dennis Bergkamp
17. Arsenal's manager between 1953-1958

G	H	F	T	W	S	R	B	F	F	A	F	I	C	L	S	K	U	X	R
L	W	C	Z	C	E	T	A	B	B	J	N	A	X	R	G	V	T	R	E
O	Y	N	R	O	R	F	B	I	U	F	K	Y	B	T	V	K	K	F	C
L	Z	F	P	Y	I	S	L	X	W	C	P	A	K	R	H	V	B	C	P
Z	U	B	R	V	P	A	I	I	I	R	K	O	L	C	E	J	Y	T	Q
G	X	N	P	H	S	A	L	G	R	M	K	I	F	Z	Q	G	H	Q	L
D	E	E	D	W	W	S	A	X	Q	B	F	E	N	B	P	G	A	U	L
H	Z	E	I	L	O	W	P	U	G	W	T	A	Y	G	I	N	W	S	E
U	D	C	L	N	I	W	M	P	Q	V	H	T	H	R	H	K	H	O	B
W	I	I	A	G	J	Q	K	A	Q	O	G	Z	W	R	Z	A	Z	T	P
Z	O	R	N	O	S	M	A	I	L	L	I	W	B	P	D	F	M	M	M
I	C	O	Z	R	Y	B	D	G	A	X	R	H	M	F	O	K	R	O	A
R	Q	O	H	D	G	L	A	J	Q	L	W	I	O	U	S	Q	W	F	C
X	M	H	Q	T	D	D	D	K	Z	D	L	T	R	I	J	G	G	D	J
X	D	O	A	R	I	E	I	V	J	H	A	T	X	C	I	E	V	W	Y
T	X	R	M	I	U	M	A	I	Q	G	E	A	I	M	H	H	O	Y	Q
U	K	B	U	M	K	D	S	Q	X	E	J	K	Q	G	Q	A	W	J	O
I	C	D	W	C	W	I	U	F	N	N	T	E	E	D	I	H	A	U	L
X	D	H	V	A	R	U	D	X	Z	D	V	R	M	2	0	0	4	O	L
E	M	Y	C	L	L	T	M	C	B	D	R	A	A	G	E	D	O	M	A

Crossword 19

1. Current Arsenal left-back, wears the number 35 shirt
2. Former Arsenal midfielder, famous for his volley against Newcastle in 2002
3. Current Arsenal centre-back pairing
4. Year in which Arsenal won their first League Cup
5. Former Arsenal manager, in charge from 1958-1962
6. Former Arsenal striker, known for his powerful left foot and goalscoring record
7. Top scorer for Arsenal in the 1998 Double-winning season
8. Arsenal player who scored the winning goal in the 2015 FA Cup Final
9. Current Arsenal striker, wears the number 9 shirt
10. Decade in which Arsenal won their first European Cup Winners' Cup
11. Arsenal player who scored the winning goal in the 1987 League Cup Final
12. Former Arsenal defender, known for his versatility and ability to play the back line
13. Nickname given to Arsenal in the 1930s due to their financial stability
14. Location of Arsenal's current training ground
15. Former Arsenal midfielder, known for his goalscoring ability from midfield
16. Former Arsenal striker, known for his acrobatic goal celebrations
17. Arsenal's manager between 1947-1953

M	Q	S	L	L	Z	Y	U	D	R	J	J	N	Z	Y	R	N	E	H	O
D	K	J	O	A	V	U	L	B	Z	R	U	E	N	O	N	R	X	H	N
L	L	A	N	I	N	E	T	E	E	N	C	L	V	F	M	V	T	M	C
W	Z	N	D	A	M	V	S	R	Z	N	G	A	Y	S	U	S	E	J	T
Z	A	V	O	K	Y	S	R	I	W	A	X	T	V	W	Q	H	O	J	C
Y	G	L	N	F	W	G	A	B	R	I	E	L	C	L	U	F	K	J	M
H	W	V	C	A	S	W	T	O	B	I	M	T	K	I	F	J	N	Z	O
S	X	E	O	O	M	P	P	D	M	X	H	Y	T	E	N	Y	E	B	S
J	E	O	L	G	T	Y	T	I	G	W	L	M	L	Y	O	I	H	S	D
V	D	B	N	B	K	T	E	G	O	D	V	F	A	I	V	W	C	A	D
H	U	G	E	J	E	G	T	S	W	W	P	F	O	O	J	V	N	L	P
Y	Z	P	Y	R	D	C	G	U	A	U	K	P	Z	D	J	P	I	V	M
Z	W	G	C	A	G	E	K	H	H	F	L	W	Y	U	K	N	Z	G	O
J	L	H	D	S	K	K	1	Q	S	J	X	G	L	L	W	X	U	O	F
V	X	M	G	S	N	P	A	9	H	N	O	S	R	E	M	C	W	H	T
N	P	K	U	I	I	G	M	M	8	B	R	F	U	A	Y	M	B	A	V
N	S	G	G	W	S	L	P	W	P	7	O	P	A	G	Y	S	Y	N	E
S	W	M	A	P	D	X	R	P	V	B	R	N	I	D	N	I	W	S	W
O	N	D	S	E	L	A	N	E	L	K	A	R	Z	D	V	M	A	J	C
Y	K	E	T	B	A	N	K	O	F	E	N	G	L	A	N	D	B	X	P

Crossword 20

1. Current Arsenal winger, wears the number 7 shirt
2. Former Arsenal goalkeeper, known for his consistency and reliability
3. Current Arsenal central midfield pairing
4. Year in which Arsenal completed an unbeaten Premier League season
5. Former Arsenal manager, in charge from 1962-1966
6. Former Arsenal striker, known for his clinical finishing and composure
7. Arsenal's captain in the 2004 Invincibles season
8. Arsenal player who scored the winning goal in the 2003 FA Cup Final
9. Current Arsenal midfielder, wears the number 20 shirt
10. Number of Premier League titles won by Arsenal
11. Arsenal player who scored the winning goal in the 1991 title-winning season
12. Former Arsenal defender, known for his aerial ability and goalscoring prowess
13. Arsenal's first ever manager
14. Arsenal's current women's captain
15. Former Arsenal midfielder, known for his passing range and vision
16. Former Arsenal striker, known for his partnership with Dennis Bergkamp
17. Arsenal's manager between 1953-1958

K	B	I	I	S	C	V	Y	U	Y	Y	R	A	G	G	K	E	S	B	F
C	Y	D	G	U	B	D	I	J	Q	I	R	O	J	U	P	A	U	D	E
L	V	S	W	L	N	R	M	J	H	N	J	D	F	M	F	V	I	Z	F
T	P	B	F	U	B	K	I	O	M	V	S	A	K	A	H	F	V	N	S
Q	K	4	R	C	A	M	P	B	E	L	L	T	Y	K	I	Z	X	W	N
T	V	Q	0	P	D	S	I	N	I	G	Z	Z	J	F	G	A	X	O	P
S	S	F	M	0	T	U	W	T	C	F	A	B	R	E	G	A	S	T	E
C	O	L	F	V	2	P	E	S	Y	N	N	E	U	M	M	M	C	J	E
C	J	M	C	K	T	H	R	E	E	G	S	J	T	Q	A	S	T	W	Y
T	P	B	J	G	R	X	A	R	Q	B	U	C	K	I	N	G	H	A	M
Q	E	I	T	K	W	F	D	I	T	H	G	L	L	A	V	I	G	E	M
F	L	R	R	A	P	D	T	P	J	N	H	L	M	N	T	F	K	U	L
M	A	M	N	A	Q	I	M	F	Y	K	I	L	D	T	J	V	I	D	A
Z	R	C	D	Y	N	O	S	L	I	W	O	J	A	H	J	M	X	Z	H
P	J	T	L	V	I	E	I	R	A	Y	E	K	F	G	H	Y	T	O	E
T	Q	H	H	M	B	L	K	G	S	U	E	K	J	I	L	Q	Y	P	N
K	S	G	C	I	G	M	Z	R	H	R	Q	T	P	R	B	C	P	V	R
E	D	I	G	K	S	M	U	S	M	I	T	H	R	W	C	X	T	L	Y
C	U	R	M	W	W	H	I	C	U	D	M	Z	J	A	T	M	B	K	R
E	M	W	K	E	J	O	R	G	I	N	H	O	U	O	P	Z	U	X	J

Answer Key

Crossword 1

1. HENRY
2. EMIRATES
3. WENGER
4. GUNNERS
5. ROSICKY
6. SPURS
7. VIEIRA
8. PI RES
9. LEHMANN
10. HIGHBURY
11. HENRY
12. FAHEY
13. 1886
14. EMERY
15. CAZORLA
16. THOMAS
17. EIDEVALL

Crossword 2

1. ARTETA
2. WALCOTT
3. RICE
4. HIGHBURY
5. WINTERBURN
6. ODEGAARD
7. LEHMANN
8. RAMSEY
9. ODEGAARD
10. O'LEARY
11. AUBAMEYANG
12. GRAHAM
13. ADAMS
14. ADIDAS
15. WILSHERE
16. WELBECK
17. WENGER

Crossword 3

1. WALCOTT
2. LJUNGBERG
3. ZINCHENKO
4. NEILL
5. PI RES
6. 1931
7. EMIRATES
8. PARLOUR
9. LEHMANN
10. MAY
11. CHARLTON

Crossword 4

1. HENRY
2. SAGNA
3. WHITE
4. 2006
5. MEE
6. ANELKA
7. ADAMS
8. PI RES
9. SMITH ROWE
10. NINETEEN
11. WRIGHT

12. ADAMS
13. FA CUP
14. ADIDAS
15. VIEIRA
16. BERGKAMP
17. CHAPMAN

12. VIEIRA
13. THE GUNNERS
14. VISIT RWANDA
15. LIMPAR
16. BOULD
17. RIOCH

Crossword 5

1. SAKA
2. SEAMAN
3. SALIBA
4. ARTETA
5. PETIT
6. 1994
7. MANOR GROUND
8. BERGKAMP
9. NKETIAH
10. FOURTEEN
11. SUNDERLAND
12. WINTERBURN
13. JVC
14. RAMSDALE
15. OVERMARS
16. BERGKAMP
17. ALLISON

Crossword 6

1. DICKS
2. BERGKAMP
3. JESUS
4. 1987
5. SWINDIN
6. HENRY
7. ANELKA
8. WALCOTT
9. JESUS
10. NINETEEN
11. MERSON
12. KEOWN
13. BANK OF ENGLAND
14. LONDON COLNEY
15. EDU
16. WELBECK
17. SHAW

Crossword 7

1. MARTINELLI
2. WILSON
3. PARTEY, RICE
4. 2004
5. WRIGHT
6. HENRY
7. VIEIRA
8. PI RES

Crossword 8

1. ODEGAARD
2. LEHMANN
3. MARTINELLI
4. 1993
5. HOWE
6. OVERMARS
7. ADAMS
8. VIEIRA

9. JORGINHO
10. THREE
11. SMITH
12. CAMPBELL
13. WHITTAKER
14. WILLIAMSON
15. FABREGAS
16. WRIGHT
17. BUCKINGHAM

9. WHITE
10. THIRTEEN
11. OVERMARS
12. ADAMS
13. PLUMSTEAD COMMON
14. JEREMY ROYLE
15. CAZORLA
16. ADAMS
17. WHITTAKER

Crossword 9

1. RAMSDALE
2. BERGKAMP
3. ZINCHENKO
4. 1993
5. KNIGHTON
6. DRAKE
7. HENRY
8. RAMSEY
9. JORGINHO
10. NINETEEN
11. DICKS
12. BOULD
13. GUNNERSAURUS REX
14. ARSENAL FOUNDATION
15. HLEB
16. HENRY
17. HENRY

Crossword 10

1. TOMIYASU
2. LEHMANN
3. GABRIEL
4. 1994
5. NEILL
6. HENRY
7. VIEIRA
8. AUBAMEYANG
9. VIERA
10. TWENTY
11. RAMSEY
12. ADAMS
13. FA CUP
14. VISIT RWANDA
15. LJUNGBERG
16. BERGKAMP
17. CHAPMAN

Crossword 11

1. PI RES
2. VIEIRA

Crossword 12

1. NKETIAH
2. LEHMANN

3. WHITE
4. 2006
5. MEE
6. WRIGHT
7. ADAMS
8. SUNDERLAND
9. SAKA
10. NINETEEN
11. ANELKA
12. CAMPBELL
13. THE GUNNERS
14. EIDEVALL
15. LIMPAR
16. BOULD
17. RIOCH

3. PARTEY
4. 1998
5. GRAHAM
6. HENRY
7. ADAMS
8. RAMSEY
9. KIWIOR
10. THIRTEEN
11. PI RES
12. ADAMS
13. FA CUP
14. VISIT RWANDA
15. LJUNGBERG
16. BERGKAMP
17. CHAPMAN

Crossword 13

1. SMITH
2. PI RES
3. ZINCHENKO
4. 1993
5. KNIGHTON
6. DRAKE
7. HENRY
8. WALCOTT
9. JORGINHO
10. NINETEEN
11. DICKS
12. BOULD
13. GUNNERSAURUS REX
14. ARSENAL FOUNDATION
15. HLEB
16. HENRY
17. HENRY

Crossword 14

1. RAMSDALE
2. BERGKAMP
3. SALIBA
4. 1994
5. NEILL
6. HENRY
7. VIEIRA
8. AUBAMEYANG
9. VIERA
10. TWENTY
11. RAMSEY
12. ADAMS
13. FA CUP
14. ADIDAS
15. LJUNGBERG
16. BERGKAMP
17. CHAPMAN

Crossword 15

1. PI RES
2. VIEIRA
3. WHITE
4. 2006
5. MEE
6. WRIGHT
7. ADAMS
8. SUNDERLAND
9. SAKA
10. NINETEEN
11. ANELKA
12. CAMPBELL
13. THE GUNNERS
14. EIDEVALL
15. LIMPAR
16. BOULD
17. RIOCH

Crossword 16

1. ELNENY
2. DICKS
3. RAMSDALE
4. 1994
5. GRAHAM
6. BERGKAMP
7. ADAMS
8. VIEIRA
9. GABRIEL
10. SEVENTY-THREE
11. OVERMARS
12. KEOWN
13. PLUMSTEAD COMMON
14. EIDEVALL
15. CAZORLA
16. ADAMS
17. WHITTAKER

Crossword 17

1. JORGINHO
2. SEAMAN
3. JESUS
4. 1993
5. HOWE
6. OVERMARS
7. ADAMS
8. VIEIRA
9. WHITE
10. THREE
11. OVERMARS
12. ADAMS
13. PLUMSTEAD

Crossword 18

1. ODEGAARD
2. WILSON
3. RICE
4. 2004
5. WRIGHT
6. HENRY
7. VIEIRA
8. PI RES
9. SALIBA
10. FOURTEEN
11. SMITH
12. CAMPBELL
13. WHITTAKER

COMMON 14. JEREMY ROYLE 15. CAZORLA 16. ADAMS 17. HENRY	14. WILLIAMSON 15. FABREGAS 16. WRIGHT 17. BUCKINGHAM
Crossword 19 1. ZINCHENKO 2. BERGKAMP 3. GABRIEL 4. 1987 5. SWINDIN 6. HENRY 7. ANELKA 8. WALCOTT 9. JESUS 10. NINETEEN 11. MERSON 12. KEOWN 13. BANK OF ENGLAND 14. LONDON COLNEY 15. EDU 16. WELBECK 17. SHAW	Crossword 20 1. SAKA 2. WILSON 3. PARTEY 4. 2004 5. WRIGHT 6. HENRY 7. VIEIRA 8. PI RES 9. JORGINHO 10. THREE 11. SMITH 12. CAMPBELL 13. WHITTAKER 14. WILLIAMSON 15. FABREGAS 16. WRIGHT 17. BUCKINGHAM

Notebook Prompt: Use this space to jot down any new facts about football you learned from this section or ideas to share with other fans. You can also jot down any questions you have about these rules or how they apply in different game situations.

....

....

....

....

....

....

....

....

....

....

....

....

....

....

....

....

CHAPTER 9

Fill in the Blanks

1. Arsenal was founded in ____.
2. The Invincibles achieved their unbeaten season in the year ____.
3. The player who scored in the 2014 FA Cup Final comeback win was ____.
4. Arsenal's all-time top goalscorer is ____.
5. ____ is Arsenal's current manager.
6. Arsenal's home ground is the ____ Stadium.
7. ____ was Arsenal's manager from 1996 to 2018.
8. Arsenal's North London rivals are ____.
9. ____ was the captain of the Invincibles.
10. ____ is Arsenal's record signing as of November 2024.
11. Arsenal won their first league title in ____.
12. ____ scored the winning goal in the 1971 Double-winning season.
13. ____ is Arsenal's current kit manufacturer.
14. ____ is Arsenal's all-time leading scorer in the Premier League.
15. The year Arsenal moved to Emirates Stadium was ____.
16. ____ scored a hat-trick against Tottenham Hotspur in 1993.
17. ____ is Arsenal's current sleeve sponsor.
18. ____ scored the winning goal in the 1993 FA Cup Final replay.
19. ____ was Arsenal's manager from 1958 to 1962.
20. ____ is Arsenal's top scorer in the 1998 Double-winning season.
21. ____ scored the winning goal in the 1987 League Cup Final.

22. ____ is Arsenal's current training ground.
23. ____ scored a hat-trick in the 2003 FA Cup Final.
24. ____ was Arsenal's manager from 1966 to 1976.
25. ____ is Arsenal's record appearance maker in the Premier League.
26. ____ scored a hat-trick against Tottenham Hotspur in 1996.
27. ____ is Arsenal's current women's manager.
28. ____ is Arsenal's current number 14.
29. ____ was Arsenal's manager from 1986 to 1995.
30. ____ is Arsenal's captain in the 1998 Double-winning season.
31. ____ scored a hat-trick in the 1991 title-winning season.
32. ____ is Arsenal's mascot.
33. ____ is Arsenal's official charity.
34. ____ is Arsenal's current number 1.
35. ____ was Arsenal's manager from 1919 to 1925.
36. ____ is Arsenal's top scorer in all competitions.
37. ____ scored the winning goal in the 2017 FA Cup Final.
38. ____ scored the winning goal in the 1993 FA Cup Final.
39. ____ was Arsenal's manager between 1947 and 1953.
40. ____ is Arsenal's current number 23.
41. ____ is Arsenal's captain in the 2002 Double-winning season.
42. ____ scored the winning goal in the 2020 FA Cup Final.
43. ____ scored the winning goal in the 2014 FA Cup Final.
44. ____ is Arsenal's first major trophy win after World War II.
45. ____ is Arsenal's current number 7.
46. ____ was Arsenal's manager from 1962 to 1966.
47. ____ is Arsenal's captain in the 2004 Invincibles season.
48. ____ scored the winning goal in the 1979 FA Cup Final.
49. ____ is Arsenal's current women's captain.
50. ____ is Arsenal's current number 10.
51. ____ is Arsenal's home ground before moving to Highbury.
52. ____ is Arsenal's current stadium announcer.
53. ____ is Arsenal's all-time top scorer in European

competitions.

54. ____ was Arsenal's first Double-winning captain.
55. ____ is Arsenal's current number 18.
56. ____ was Arsenal's manager from 1976 to 1983.
57. ____ is Arsenal's current number 8.
58. ____ is Arsenal's manager between 1953 and 1958.
59. ____ is Arsenal's current number 2.
60. ____ was Arsenal's manager from 1915 to 1919.
61. ____ is Arsenal's current number 21.
62. ____ was Arsenal's manager between 1939 and 1945.
63. ____ is Arsenal's current number 4.
64. ____ is Arsenal's first ever manager.
65. ____ is Arsenal's all-time appearance maker.
66. ____ is Arsenal's current number 11.
67. ____ is Arsenal's current first-choice goalkeeper.
68. ____ is Arsenal's former manager, known for his "boring, boring Arsenal" quote.
69. ____ is Arsenal's record appearance maker in the Premier League.
70. ____ is the number of goals scored by Arsenal in the 2003-04 "Invincibles" season.
71. ____ is the location of Arsenal's current training ground.
72. ____ is the nickname given to Arsenal in the 1930s due to their financial stability.
73. ____ is the decade in which Arsenal won their first League Cup.
74. ____ is the year in which Arsenal won their first FA Cup double.
75. ____ is the number of FA Cup final appearances by Arsenal.
76. ____ is the number of trophies won by Arsène Wenger as Arsenal manager.
77. ____ is the former Arsenal midfielder, known for his "Invincibles" goal against Liverpool.

78. ____ is the former Arsenal striker, known for his "twisted blood" celebration.
79. ____ is the former Arsenal midfielder, known for his technical ability and passing range.
80. ____ is the former Arsenal defender, known for his partnership with Tony Adams.
81. ____ is the former Arsenal defender, known for his tough tackling and disciplinary record.
82. ____ is the former Arsenal midfielder, known for his creativity and passing ability.
83. ____ is the former Arsenal striker, known for his "one-nil to the Arsenal" chant.
84. ____ is the former Arsenal goalkeeper, known for his penalty-saving abilities in the 2003 FA Cup Final.
85. ____ is the former Arsenal defender, known for his tough tackling and no-nonsense approach.
86. ____ is the former Arsenal goalkeeper, known for his consistency and reliability.
87. ____ is the former Arsenal defender, known for his aerial ability and goalscoring prowess.
88. ____ is the former Arsenal midfielder, known for his passing range and vision.
89. ____ is the former Arsenal striker, known for his partnership with Dennis Bergkamp.
90. ____ is the former Arsenal goalkeeper, known for his shot-stopping ability and reflexes.
91. ____ is the former Arsenal striker, known for his pace and dribbling skills.
92. ____ is the former Arsenal midfielder, known for his goalscoring ability from midfield.
93. ____ is the former Arsenal striker, known for his acrobatic goal celebrations.
94. ____ is the former Arsenal goalkeeper, known for his eccentric personality and saves.

95. ____ is the former Arsenal striker, known for his clinical finishing and composure.
96. ____ is the former Arsenal striker, known for his powerful left foot and goalscoring record.
97. ____ is the former Arsenal striker, known for his partnership with Ian Wright.
98. ____ is the former Arsenal midfielder, known for his volley against Newcastle in 2002.
99. ____ is the former Arsenal midfielder, known for his powerful shots and long-range goals.
100. ____ is the former Arsenal striker, known for his pace and clinical finishing.

Answers (in order):

1. 1886
2. 2004
3. Ramsey
4. Thierry Henry
5. Mikel Arteta
6. Emirates
7. Arsène Wenger
8. Tottenham Hotspur
9. Patrick Vieira
10. Declan Rice
11. 1931
12. Ray Kennedy
13. Adidas
14. Thierry Henry
15. 2006
16. Ian Wright
17. Visit Rwanda
18. Andy Linighan
19. George Swindin
20. Nicolas Anelka
21. Charlie Nicholas
22. London Colney
23. Robert Pires
24. Bertie Mee
25. David O'Leary
26. Nicolas Anelka
27. Jonas Eidevall
28. Eddie Nketiah
29. George Graham
30. Tony Adams
31. Alan Smith
32. Gunnersaurus Rex

33. The Arsenal Foundation
34. Aaron Ramsdale
35. Leslie Knighton
36. Thierry Henry
37. Aaron Ramsey
38. Andy Linighan
39. Tom Whittaker
40. Takehiro Tomiyasu
41. Patrick Vieira
42. Pierre-Emerick Aubameyang
43. Aaron Ramsey
44. FA Cup
45. Bukayo Saka
46. Billy Wright
47. Patrick Vieira
48. Alan Sunderland
49. Kim Little
50. Martin Ødegaard
51. Plumstead Common
52. Jeremy Royle
53. Thierry Henry
54. Tony Adams
55. Gabriel Jesus
56. Terry Neill
57. Jorginho
58. George Swindin
59. Jakub Kiwior
60. Leslie Knighton
61. Fabio Vieira
62. George Allison
63. Ben White
64. Thomas Mitchell
65. David O'Leary

66. Gabriel Martinelli
67. Aaron Ramsdale
68. George Graham
69. David O'Leary
70. 73
71. London Colney
72. Bank of England
73. 1980s (1987)
74. 1993
75. 20
76. 13
77. Dennis Bergkamp
78. Thierry Henry
79. Alexander Hleb
80. Steve Bould
81. Martin Keown
82. Santi Cazorla
83. Tony Adams
84. David Seaman
85. Tony Adams
86. Bob Wilson
87. Sol Campbell
88. Cesc Fàbregas
89. Ian Wright
90. Jens Lehmann
91. Marc Overmars
92. Edu
93. Danny Welbeck
94. Jens Lehmann
95. Thierry Henry
96. Thierry Henry
97. Dennis Bergkamp
98. Dennis Bergkamp

99. Freddie Ljungberg
100. Thierry Henry

Notebook Prompt: Use this space to jot down any new facts about football you learned from this section or ideas to share with other fans. You can also jot down any questions you have about these rules or how they apply in different game situations.

....

....

....

....

....

....

....

....

....

....

....

....

....

....

....

....

CONCLUSION